# Embrace Your Divine Flow

## Evolvements for Healing

# Embrace Your Divine Flow

## Evolvements for Healing

*Editors* JULIAN HOBSON, BHSC CHt &
LORENE SHYBA, MFA PhD
*Art* HELENA HADALA, MFA RCA
*Foreword* ELIZABETH ROCKENBACH BIP

UPROUTE IMPRINT OF DURVILE & UPROUTE BOOKS
CALGARY, ALBERTA, CANADA
DURVILE.COM

*Scan to interact with the book and authors.*

*Durvile.com*

Durvile Publications Ltd.

UPROUTE IMPRINT OF DURVILE AND UPROUTE BOOKS

Calgary, Alberta, Canada
www.durvile.com



LIBRARY AND ARCHIVES CATALOGUING IN PUBLICATIONS DATA

Embrace Your Divine Flow: Evolvements for Healing
Hobson, Julian: Editor
Shyba, Lorene: Editor
Hadala, Helena: Artist
Rockenbach, Elizabeth: Foreword

1. Wellbeing | 2. Spirituality | 3. Canadian Literature | 4. Canadian Art
5. Healing | 6. Body Mind Spirit

The UpRoute Every River Lit Series, "Ways of Light" Title

ISBN: 978-1-990735-09-7 (print pbk) | ISBN: 978-1-990735-41-7 (ebook)
ISBN: 978-1-990735-42-4 (audio)

The following stories are republished from Durvile's UpRoute Imprint books:

Mountain, Antoine, "Spirits of the Departed" are excerpts from
*Child of Morning Star: Embers of an Ancient Dawn.* 2023.
Soop Alex, "Niisitapi Reveal," from *Midnight Sun Moonless Sky.* 2014.
Original Title, "A Lively Old Merriment." Story Revised.
Yakeleya, Raymond, "The Mountain, the Wind and the Wildflower,"
from *The Tree by the Woodpile.* 2017.

Cover art: Helena Hadala RCA, *Transformation* | Book design: Lorene Shyba

We acknowledge the traditional land of the Treaty 7 Peoples of Southern Alberta: the Siksika, Piikani, and Kainai of the Niisitapi (Blackfoot) Confederacy; the Dene Tsuut'ina; and the Chiniki, Bearspaw, and Wesley Stoney Nakoda First Nations and the Region 3 Métis Nation of Alberta.

Durvile Publications gratefully acknowledges the financial support of The Government of Canada through Canadian Heritage, Canada Book Fund and the Government of Alberta, Alberta Media Fund.

Printed and bound in Canada. Second Printing. 2023.

This book is a dedication
of love
to all our
friends and families,
in presence and in absence.

*— the editors and authors*

## CONTENTS

## CONTENTS

FOREWORD

# THE POWER OF PARABLE

*Elizabeth Rockenbach*

## OPENING PRAYER

We are free as Fire is free. We flow as Water flows.
Our bodies vibrate with the Earth and
we breathe the same sacred Air.
We are not bound by past experiences,
our habitual patterns, or an unknown future.
We walk together, free of all that would limit us.
We were created unbound and live in
a state of pure spiritual freedom.
The abundance of Spirit flows in and through us.
We are channels for self-love,
self-acceptance, and self-forgiveness.
This is the Power of Parable
The Power of Evolvement.

PARABLE IS A RIVER flowing beneath our human experience. Making sense of the world through parables, or 'evolvements', is as timeless as human language. These story evolvements are rooted in oral traditions, the written word, hand gestures and facial expressions, movement, and visual representations. They explore different ways humans make meaning in our lives across generations. Some authors work through creation stories, while others tell tales of our demise. Scaffolding these written pieces are the gorgeous and expressive paintings of Helena Hadala.

*Embrace Your Divine Flow* is more than a book of powerful stories and pictures. The authors and editors have created exercises so that the reader may apply the lessons in their own lives. It is through lived experience that we connect ourselves to community, art, and spirituality. A multitude of approaches are represented here including Mindfulness, emotional exploration through the senses, Buddhist *Chod* practice of overcoming the ego, storytelling, prayers of gratitude, poetry, visual art, sound and vibrational healing.

I felt called to write this foreword because of an energetic connection to the title and intention of the work *Embrace Your Divine Flow.* The opportunity arose at a time when I was making another big change in my life, having relocated to a small remote town in New Mexico, and it had everything to do with Divine flow!

My ancestors were farmers, but I had never been on an actual farm until I took an apprenticeship on a market vegetable farm as a young adult. It was the ideal place for me to put my hands in the earth and watch as seeds sprouted into plants, and plants bore fruit. After a few years of intensive physical labour my back became unable to support me in this work any longer. I turned to natural ways to heal my spine. Thus began the journey I have been on for twenty years of healing the mind and body.

I studied energy healing at the Barbara Brennan School of Healing. The school's founder, and my brilliant teacher, Barbara Brennan, developed a healing science that supports us as human beings to heal our emotional and spiritual wounds and to manifest the life that we want. Barbara Brennan was a scientist as well as a mystic. She grounded her studies of the human energy field with her background in physics and believed that in unlocking our emotional wounds, we would find our greatest gifts.

I opened to the reality that all physical disease is a manifestation of a complex matrix of our emotions, thoughts and beliefs, experiences, and relationship to the whole universe and all its elements. My physical injuries healed. I connect to these following evolvement parables and exercises because the artist and authors not only accept this truth of our Divine nature, but also offer a range of ways to work with this kind of practical magic.

Eventually, I began to feel the call of nature again. I needed to get out of the city and firmly replant myself on the earth. Divine guidance led me to an internet search of a tiny town just outside the vast magnificent Gila Wilderness. Here I found the most unusual posting. Instead of the typical list of square footage, number of bedrooms and bathrooms, and other amenities, this post was written in a narrative format. It told of magic, fairies, of a creek that flows among a high desert terrain, and a charming little house that sits among the sunflowers.

I spoke to my niece, who, at the time, was spending long afternoons with me. "This is my house!" I showed her the beauty that was calling to me, and from that moment on, I referred to it only as "My Sunflower Home." Two years later, I am living here, in my sunflower house amongst the mountains and juniper.

~

I FIND A LOT OF RESONANCE with Rich Théroux's "Let the World Catch Up" where the narrator has a knack for making wishes come true. In his story he sees through pictures, as the wish granters do not speak, but they do see. As long as the narrator believes what he is saying, it is so.

For me, there is immense healing through exploring and regulating my energy field. Much like Marty and Jake find in Lorene Shyba's, "Aura Borealis," light and colour are essential elements in the healing process. Our auric fields contain all of the colours of the spectrum, and in this healing evolvement, the siblings find their essential nature in the Aurora Borealis with the support of a wise woman healer and guide.

The human experience is at times painful, difficult to understand, and baffling. A saving grace in these moments of suffering is the surrender to a Divine flow. We long to connect to a greater force than ourselves, whether that be Love, community, the elements, God, *Newet'sine,* Source, or Nature. We discover ourselves and an elegant meaning to life through Art and Expression. These authors have poured their understanding of the Force of their art into their stories that they have shared here.

Our own personal timelines may seem haphazard as we live our lives moment to moment. Revelations come, we live through their magic, and we return time and again to a feeling that living can put us in real danger. As in Mar'ce Merrell's "Water Calls, Water Holds," sometimes we have to enter an unsteady vessel and live through the fear with only our brave hearts to sustain us. She guides us through her practice of 'feeding your demons', employing stillness, imagination, sketching, and movement to overcome the ego.

All healing is embodied. Our human vessels give us the ability to evolve and transform. Sensation and the present moment are keystones to Valerie Campbell's "Moving her Poetic Body," where breath and the spiritual tradition of *Anam Cara* moves the narrator's body and pen to create poetry. In her workshop exercises, Campbell explores the unconscious through authentic movement and a writing practice.

Another balm for our soul in challenging times are sacred places. Yellow Horn and Yakeleya explore this terrain in their stories. Iikiinayoonaa Marlene Yellow Horn offers us a traditional Napii story in "Sacred Places" that is part of the Blackfoot creation myth. She discovers the only real quality that matters in a tale is Truth. Community unites us.

Raymond Yakeleya's "The Mountain, the Wind, and the Wildflowers," takes us on a trek to find the essence of *Newet'sine* the Creator in nature that is all around us—in the places that we cannot see, like the wind and beauty that is knowable to the eye, such as beautiful wildflowers.

As healing has become a way of being in my life, I have aligned with a group of the most open-hearted and open-minded people I have known. We have formed Universal Healing, an online forum for group energy healing, from a spiritual download that a dear colleague had in service of global healing. We experience the joy of making healing accessible to everyone, anywhere on the planet. A revelation we have with each healing is sacred alignment and community. It feels like, as a soloist, I have become a member of a divine orchestra. Instead of working alone, we join in concert with each other and with our clients and their spiritual support, such as ancestors and divine guides. There are no bounds to this venture, and I am ever grateful to live at this edge of evolving.

Group work allows the healing field to be magnified by the collective energy. It is why monks meditate together. This is, in my opinion, what brought these authors and artist together in this Divine embrace awaiting you. Individuals long for community to express and hold the power of Life and Story. Here, the invitation to you is to practice the wisdom that is called forth through story. Please join with us to embrace the evolution of humanity.

Spirit has guided me back to the earth, to my own little place in the mountains of New Mexico, where I fell in love with rainbows, sublime skies, and the alluring smell of juniper. Here, I have fertile land around me to inspire my dream of healing our planet.

We hope these stories and exercises guide you to ask these questions. What is your relationship to Nature? What is your Art? What is your unique Medicine? How does the Divine flow through you?

— *Elizabeth Rockenbach*
*Co-Founder Universal-Healing.org*

*Elizabeth facilitates a client's intrinsic and natural ability to heal body, mind,and spirit. She works one on one, in group settings, workshops, classes, and through writing. In addition to her niece, Leah, mentioned in this foreword, Elizabeth adores her nephew Eli, especially while playing* Mad Libs *together. She recalls often his wisdom, when, at an early age he asked: "How will you know how someone feels unless you ask them?"*

## INTRODUCTION

# SHARED DYNAMICS

*Julian Hobson and Lorene Shyba*

### VERISIMILITUDE

VERISIMILITUDE is a way for us to explain and honour the way the stories and images in *Embrace Your Divine Flow* have evolved from a longing for expression of metaphorical truths. At the genesis of this book, we asked authors to write about their connection to the divine and they created rich and compelling 'evolvements' or parables that take place through many eras. Authors experimented with narrative styles, drilling down into their spiritual wisdom that sometimes, by surprise, emerged unintentionally but always with genuine verisimilitude—the quality of appearing to be true or real. Well-fleshed and often-quirky, unusual characters evolved, with plot journeys that progressed toward a point of inspiration about one particular, focused theme.

As an example of personal truths emerging unintentionally, we were enchanted to hear Audrya Chancellor tell us, "I love my story and am in awe that it came through me," John Heerema's disclosure that his ending came as "quite the surprise," and Islene Runningdeer telling us that "my writing flows ... and at times what emerges isn't necessarily recalled." These are voices, expressing truth through a high level of intuition and divine flow. In a haiku that accompanies her image *Boundaries*, Helena Hadala also shares an insight about extra-sensory intuition:

Whispers of silence
Unravel mysteries
Listen with intent

Drawn from life into these pages, in her story "Tough Love," Lynda Partridge writes about transitioning from human world trauma to dreamworld and back again to a peaceful compromise. Similarly, in "The Veil," Kayla Lappin guides us to security and protection that she herself may have traversed. She says, "You are not lost; you are not broken. You cannot move into the place of security until the water has poured over your hands and spilled from your soul. All must be allowed to shine forth."

## PEACE

*Our special life is one of a kind and these moments can never be repeated. We continue forward into our next moment and evolve as we learn with our divine gifts, our divine tools, and our divine guidance flowing through us. Embrace it all. Peace.*

We can experience unconditional love, neutrality, observation, love without condition — no ego, no pain, no suffering, no conditioning, no programming. This is also known as peace—floating in the peace of love and protection, perfectly, as before birth and as after the death of the body.

This floating peace is achievable after the moment of birth and before the moment of death, but it takes practice, discipline, and dedication. It is part of our evolvement to endure the practice the dedication, and the discipline.

The attainment of peace in life will not always be successful. We will be programmed and conditioned to different degrees, but we can overcome it. However, we can adapt and improvise to help us feel the true peace we search for. Along the way there will be pain and suffering but we can know that our tools for peace, available to us as gifts, are already inside us. These tools are waiting for their moment to be picked up and utilized for our own unique benefit.

## THE ART AND EXERCISES

*"If you want to find the secrets of the universe, think in terms of energy, frequency and vibration." —Nikola Tesla*

Helena Hadala's artworks in the book, the 18 images in her Confluence series, are mirrored in the stories and in the chapter exercises. Each story, or set of stories, has been assigned an art piece that bears a significance to the content and message of the story. Besides containing glimpses of these concepts within the narrative, the first exercise after every chapter relates to a suggested activity that corresponds to the image's title and impulse. For example, our stories have been assigned the images *Breathe* (Julian's "Mother Son") and *Nothing*, (Lorene's "Aura Borealis") and our formative exercises explore breath and stillness.

Overall the exercises are achievable with dedication, discipline, and practice. At the basic level, they are simple, quick and easy—but not to be underestimated. These exercises are the light to the germinating seeds that are the special gifts inside us. They await their moment to flower or become even greater.

Believe. It's easy to just try something. If you believe, you will succeed, so just try. Have courage to exert your free will and have patience in your infinite divine flow. Realize courage is redundant because there is no fear. Find a way to separate mind, body, and soul and then reconnect at will and with varying strength. Experience your own truth, no holds barred, and feel its power.

It is only a matter of time and practice before you find out what to do to improve and evolve. Give permission for positivity, and you can choose to ignore negativity. If negativity is observed, do not give it any attention. You can choose not to talk about it.

As Nikola Tesla attests, vibration, frequency, and energy are the keys. If we discover and extrapolate this by being aware and listening, we can create a revival toward truth and true power.

Listen.

## THE POWER OF SHARING

*"We exist in this miraculous world together.*
*We have come into life to develop,*
*to share new stories ... "* — *Hilda Chasia Smith*

The power of sharing is a knowing, conscious effort to give and receive love in its many forms and the awareness and willingness to participate. This cooperation increases power by much more than the sum of its parts, like two 10-watt bulbs when added together become 100-watts, if they are ethereal.

Two souls sharing together are brighter than their individual summation. So, the power of sharing transcends physics.

*Love shared*
*beats all. Wins because*
*of the power of sharing.*
*Working together in*
*love is unbeatable.*
*Always wins.*

The power of each evolvement, when combined with the art and exercises, is exponentially increased because it is part of a shared collective of love, with intention to heal. When the exercises are combined and performed frequently and consistently, they become more powerful because of their shared sum.

*Dear reader,*
*transmit the sharing*
*and become part of the power*
*The power of sharing in relationships*
*with work colleagues, with family*
*with comrades, with animal companions*
*Sharing calmness, knowledge, and wisdom.*
*Always learning.*

The power of sharing is also protection

ONE

# WATER CALLS, WATER HOLDS

*Mar'ce Merrell*

*Water calls*
*three beings in an open vessel,*
*In and on and through an unknown expanse.*
*Water holds.*

Tara steps into the bow of the canoe: First, paddle across the gunnels, left foot in, weight shift left, butt towards seat. Second, right foot up and over and down. Third, butt in seat, brace paddle.

Despite Tara's careful movement and Sean steadying the stern, the canoe shuffles side-to-side. Unstable. Athena, the black retriever puppy jumps into her spot in the middle. Wobbling canoe, now, like a pendulum striking another pendulum.

"Athena, sit. Sit. Sit. Sit." Sean commands.

Athena senses dismay in the rain, the wind gusts, the thunder, and in Tara's fear. Tara, eyes closed, imagines a sunny sky calm day. She focuses her thoughts. *I am okay. We are okay. We are okay. I am okay.*

She opens her eyes to this: grey skies, falling rain, lightning striking in the west. Her gut numbs, hands tingle and sweat, her heart races. The canoe slips and shifts. She feels Sean step into the stern. Feels the push of his paddle moving them away from shore. She lifts her paddle into the air, extends her bottom hand, drops the blade in the water, pushes with her top hand, guides the paddle back and back, until the motion is complete, turns her hand to lessen the resistance of the exit, swings the paddle back to starting position. A few long strokes flow them into deeper water, choppier water. Southeasterly gusts hit them from the side.

They paddle away from Portage des Morts.

~

Waves rise higher and higher, crest, and break into whitecaps. Crashing waves wake all the slumbering beings below: fish, plant, sand, rock. And a presence notices. Remembers. Needs to have a conversation.

The presence gathers itself from the bottom of the lake, from the essence of all the waking beings.

This gathering of aliveness slides through gaps in the Precambrian rocks, the oldest exposed rocks on the planet, in residence since before the dinosaurs, before the first bushes or trees, before the first one-celled creatures.

The presence gathers itself. Billions and billions of spirits unite, unseen.

~

Tara wants to be brave.

She remembers her nightmares—so many nights of panic, of feeling the canoe flipping. She remembers the feeling of tossing in waves of restlessness, of falling out of bed, of waking up drenched in sweat, of gasping for breath. Still in the space between dream-time and now-time, curled up in fetal position on the floor beside the bed, she remembers the push and pull of water, the crash, the sound of something breaking. She remembers the flailing, the sucking in of deep breath. The submersion. Again. Again. These words come to her: You cannot save anyone.

She doesn't believe these words.

She has saved many people. Kindness saves. She is kind. For this reason, she doesn't tell Sean about her nightmares. She tells him about her dreams of her mother comforting her.

"Do you think the dead can talk to you?" She asks Sean.

His answer: "I think your mind can create whatever it needs in order to survive."

Tara's never considered her nightmares might be preparing her for what is to come. Until today.

~

"Fear is the mind-killer," Sean quotes from *Dune* when they paddle choppy water, "Fear is that little-death that brings total obliteration." Sean isn't afraid of the canoe tipping. He secretly fears his own death.

Sean carries his secrets deep. Given up by his mother a few months after he was born, most of his relationships end with him realizing he's trapped someone into a corner and he has to walk away to let them free. Only one has ended badly enough to haunt him.

His adopted mother died. He doesn't remember how, exactly, but he remembers his frustration, his use of force on a dark night, in a rented cottage far away from observers. Everyone blames her death on a man who'd been passing through. A man who disappeared.

After his adopted mother's death, the high school counsellor referred Sean to a psychiatrist to help him with poor concentration in his classes, declining attendance. The counsellor, a woman who looked and talked like his mother (kindly and slowly and with eyes that did not look away), told him the psychiatrist would help him bridge the gap between the life he had with his mother and the life he would now have. "A promising life." The woman fingered a gold necklace with linked letters forming the phrase: *I choose joy.*

"Wounds," the psychiatrist advised him, "must be allowed to heal. In order to heal, you must be willing to be vulnerable, to let your wounds be seen."

"I just need some drugs to help me sleep," Sean told the man with the goatee and the round glasses and piercing eyes. Since then, he's spent most of his life in the bush, on a ski slope, in a canoe. His few friends, so in awe of his skill in keeping himself and everyone else alive, accept his gruffness.

The secret underneath all the secrets, the wound at the bottom of the well?

Sean hoped only for one thing.

To be loved. Divinely. Completely.

~

Tara and Sean met at a wedding. Friends of friends invited them. A summer night under the glow of Orion and the haze of the Milky Way, the air stood still, gathered heat with each slow song, each crooned ballad.

The two of them stuck to opposite sides of the dance floor until the DJ played "Dancing With Myself" by Billy Idol. Sean led the way. The sole dancer, he sprung up and down, pogo stick-style, waving his arms, flinging his hair, calling in the wind.

As the breeze grew, Tara felt herself being sucked into a vortex of twirl and boogie and the two of them created circles moving in opposite directions, a circle inside a circle, as if building a tornado. When they crashed into each other, they fell in a heap of laughter.

Later, they watched Orion cross the sky. He talked about risking his life in snow, water, trees, and air. She talked about heartbreak, forgiveness, and love. Both motherless, both wanting love to grow fast and forever, they moved in together, bought a canoe, and adopted a puppy.

~

Athena, the puppy named after a goddess of protection, understands love as face licking, dancing between her people, and falling asleep to sweet lullabies and soft caresses. In her dreams, she is a dark shadow plunging in water, slipping on ice, bounding over boulders, sluicing through sand, galloping in long grasses, circling out and back to find Tara and Sean waiting.

The team of three is on day five of their ten-day journey through the Canadian Shield, on rivers and through lakes they've never paddled. Their choice is neither usual nor unusual. Their motivation is to stay together, no matter the grief they've been facing.

Sean is lead navigator and protector. His mind focuses on assessing danger and planning ahead. Tara offers pinches of dried sage from the prairies of Calgary, here and there, as if to say, thank you, we will tread softly. Athena regards all moments as adventures. Her acute sensory abilities reveal a deep rumbling sound, the changing smells of the lake: more fishy, more earthy, more animal.

Athena lays her head down on the bottom of the canoe, closes her eyes, tries to block out the sounds, the smells, the wind. She remembers her life before birth, tucked in her mother's womb with eight others, moving with her mother's quick and slow movements, feeling her mother's heartbeat.

~

The gathering continues metres and metres below the lake's surface. Memories and memories of memories assemble in layers, begin to find a form. The gathering is answering the calls from Sean, from Tara, from Athena.

~

Tara nearly drowned at least four times in this life, the second time happened when she was nine. She remembers eyes wide open, looking up through the water at the sky. She remembers gulping air before going down in big waves. She remembers being carried and jostled by water and being shoved, violently pushed, towards shore. (That time she was cut and bruised.) She remembers wondering how she survived and why. Now, she wonders what she is meant to do in this life. Why is she here?

Sean guards the gates of his memories with planning and assessment, with more and more movement. When he is still, he is vulnerable. When he is vulnerable, he, too, feels the mind-killer: fear. He practices his reaction time even as he paddles, shortening his strokes, switching sides to redirect the canoe. He wants Tara to focus on his skill at keeping them on course. All she has to do is paddle. And if they tip? Stay with the canoe. The canoe is their mother, Sean has told Tara over and over, we stay with the canoe, we protect the canoe. He's not worried about the waves. He's paddled much worse. Maybe they'll practice rescue scenarios later today. Maybe he'll show her how to use the knives he's attached to their life jackets, just in case they capsize, just in case they get tangled up in their ropes. All she needs is confident memories.

Athena, thirteen months old in human measurement of time, accumulates memories faster and faster each day she lives. When she smells rabbit poop, all the times she's loved the taste of rabbit poop arrive and converge in a singular ravenous moment. The taste of grass and root filtered through a bunny's belly? Undeniably exquisite. And swimming? She learned a few weeks ago her power to use her webbed feet, the sleek line of her body and tail to keep her afloat, the way her head and snout can remain above water. Land and water. To her they are equally joyous.

~

The wind surges and gusts. Waves on the water build higher, break and break in rapid and unexpected patterns.

"Woo-hoo!" Sean yells. "Time to kneel."

Tara and Sean kneel on the bottom of the canoe and lean into the oncoming wind, attempt to narrow the gap between canoe and water. They can't hold the line though, with such inconsistent wind.

Athena whimpers. Fear from the front of the canoe, from Tara, feels like waves colliding. Sean steers them into the waves at a slight angle. The canoe crests, nose high in the air, and crashes into the gap between the waves. At the top of a wave, Tara's paddle can't reach for the next pool to push into, to lever them forward. At the bottom, the canoe takes on big splashes of water.

"Paddle, Tara! Paddle!" Sean shouts. His knees slip in the water pooling in the stern of the canoe. Gust after gust after gust assails them.

Now, he struggles to keep them on course. The trim of the canoe is off for the wind they're in. Tara's too small to keep the nose down. He thought she had enough experience to handle a big-ish crossing like this. How could he have misjudged her? What disaster will he have to get them out of? Why isn't she listening?

A memory rises of him in a plane years ago, a woman, nearly twice his weight seated in front of him. When she reclined her seat, her weight came at him with so much force it snapped his tray table. A full cup of hot coffee plunged into his lap. She didn't care, not in the least. He swallowed furious anger.

When the plane landed, he stood before she could, pulled his backpack from the stowage above her and 'accidentally' swung his heavy backpack into her head. He clocked her, like a punch to the face. Nearby passengers gasped but she didn't react. Instead, she looked at him. Grey, stormy, unyielding eyes. He wanted to punch her. He wanted her to look down. He wanted her to know his needs were important.

Now he is in a canoe, paddling in manageable waves and failing because he's trusted Tara when he shouldn't have. He can't focus on what he's doing because she's a mess in the front of the canoe. Paddling sometimes, not paddling others.

"Tara! Listen! Listen to me!!" He yells. "Paddle!!"

Tara digs into the water. Digs and digs. Short strokes. She is nearly rowing with her paddle—full body forward, grab the water, pull it back. This is my nightmare. We're gonna tip. We are about to tip. We will tip.

Athena sits up, shifts from side to side in the canoe. The vessel slips dangerously in and out of Sean's control. Now, he yells at the puppy.

"Athena, sit! Sit! Lay down!"

Tara can't see what Sean sees. Sean can't see what Tara sees. Athena closes her eyes. The gathering beneath them is growing louder.

~

Old stories of large swimming creatures—lake monsters with heads the size of horses, sleek bodies, and strange tails arise around campfires all through northern Ontario. So much water, so many lakes, so many unknown creatures. Nearly thirty pictographs of canoe and moose, beaver, and bear remain on boulders high enough to reach while standing in a canoe.

Lives have changed on this water. Some have given everything away. Some have taken everything.

So many breaths. Each breath, a moment. Each moment, an event.

The presence is aware of all the breaths. The presence shapes into form based on the desire, the need. The shape of a moose head appears and along with it, the keen sense of hearing and smelling, and then the lake trout lends its skin and gills, for smooth passage, and the beaver's broad tail follows, a useful tool in battle or aid. The form grows with each breath of Tara, Sean, and Athena.

~

Tara struggles. Her shoulders burn. Switching sides offers only a few seconds of relief. Her wrists ache. The only way she can keep paddling is to breathe in, breathe out slow and hold the empty-air-in-her-lungs feeling until she can't any longer. Her neck is knotted so tight she's afraid she might rip the muscles if she turns to look at Sean behind her. Her eyes half-close.

We're going to die. We're going to die.

She paddles hard. Slacks off. Paddles hard. Inside her mind, she experiences zero safety; the warning system is past yellow and amber. Red flashes cloud her vision. The canoe moves erratically with the uneven paddling.

"Paddle! Paddle! Paddle!"

She looks around. Theirs is the only canoe on the water.

Lightning flashes closer and closer.

Someone save us. Please save us.

In the nightmare she's had, over and over, she can't save anyone, not even herself.

"Tara, focus!" Sean yells. "Listen to me!"

"Athena, sit!"

"Paddle! Tara!"

"Athena, sit!"

His voice tells her they're in the worst trouble. Deep trouble. Now, the sound of him forcing Athena to sit twists in her gut. This is the kind of trouble you don't recover from. The kind you run from. The kind that dooms you.

Sean's thoughts and Tara's thoughts converge: *Fear is the mind-killer. Fear is the little-death that brings total obliteration.*

~

It happens now. It happens now.

Tara feels the giving-up-feeling begin. She sets her paddle down across the gunnels, checks to make sure her life jacket is secure. She has emergency survival gear in the pockets, a knife attached to the front. The sky is dark with clouds. Thunder grumbles. Lightning flashes on the horizon. She squints. The white and red pine and the cedars bend with the wind, trying to hold on without breaking. The soundtrack of her mind quiets.

The water will be warm.

A rogue wave comes towards them from far down the lake. They both see the wave building, gathering, gathering, gathering. The wave races towards them. Time speeds up.

Riding on the top of the building wave, Tara notices antlers, a rack of moose antlers, attached to a massive moose head. A moose? A massive moose?

"Back paddle! Back paddle!" Sean yells.

She turns her head to try to understand what he means. Pain shoots from her right ear down into her shoulder. Sean reaches back with his paddle, stabs the water, pushes with all of his muscles to move the canoe back. Can he stop time? Can he avoid what is about to happen? His movements are all over the place. She's never seen him this panicked. The face of a man who realizes...

Athena barks. Athena barks and barks.

Tara looks forward.

The moose head rises to the top of the wave in front of them. A tsunami wave. So poor is the vision of a moose that only when they are a few metres away can they see the ones they are about to clock with their massive antlers.

She holds her paddle in the air, level with the horizon, the universal sign for STOP. The lake monster (moose/lake trout/beaver) attempts to change direction, but its momentum carries it too fast, and its size is so immense. The water swells. Tara looks into one of the moose's eyes and the moose jerks its head to look at her with the other eye.

Tara feels the monster's breath in an arc of gentle warmth. She knows just before it's too-late what they must do to avoid being sunk or squashed.

"Jump!" She yells. "Sean, Athena, jump!!!"

"Stay with the canoe!" Sean yells.

Athena jumps. Tara jumps.

Tara keeps her eyes open, inhales a full breath before she hits the water. The crash into the water is clean, but even with a life jacket on, she is pulled down and down.

She focuses her mind: Athena. Athena. Athena. She calls and calls with her mind. Sean. Sean. Sean.

The water is calm underneath the waves. And clear. She looks up. A massive shape creates a shadow above her.

She has a memory of her mother reaching into the water when she was drowning, her mother's hands cradling her neck, lifting her from the water. Her mother. Her mother. Her mother.

Now, small bubbles float from her nostrils during a slow exhale. Her lungs empty. In the gap of no-breath, she closes her eyes, allows her arms to open out wide as if she were a startled baby. She relaxes. Her right hand touches, something. She grips Athena's harness. They begin the journey upward.

~

"No!" Sean fights to stay with the canoe—tries to direct the nose to take the wave at an angle, but the wave moves suddenly, unexpectedly. The wave crashes down in the middle of the canoe, but it isn't just water that lands. No. A head and antlers of a moose crack the centre of the canoe. Sean falls forward, his head presses against an enormous nostril. When the lake monster inhales, it sucks in Sean's ear.

No way. No way am I going to die. No way.

With the propulsion of the lake monster's out breath, Sean reaches up and grabs on to one side of the moose's antlers, antlers spanning at least five metres—the entire length of the canoe. Words from memory come to him: *Fear is the mind-killer. I will face my fear. I will permit it to pass over me and through me.* He reaches for the knife attached to the outside of his life jacket and struggles to free it from the sheath.

The crack in the canoe gives way and the two halves separate. Soon he will be pulled under.

Sean's left arm grips the moose antler. His right hand holds the knife. He pulls and pulls to get himself closer to the moose's eye. A knife to the eye will change everything. Sean's will is so keen, so focused. His body is alive with the will to survive, every cell buzzes. His eye comes even with the lake monster. He feels the brush of long moose eyelashes against his cheek, smells the decomposition of billions of organisms. He pulls his right arm back, holds the knife in a stabbing position.

Words from memory come to him: *I will face my fear. I will permit it to pass over me and through me. And when it has gone past I will turn the inner eye to see its path. Where the fear has gone there will be nothing. Only I will remain.*

Reflected in the moose's eye, he sees his own face, wide-eyed with fear and tense with anger, reflected in an iris of calm. I will turn the inner eye to see its path. He lets go of the knife, grabs one last breath, holds it.

The lake monster dives, dragging still-clinging Sean to the lake bottom.

~

The lake trout body brushes Tara and Athena, both of them submerged but rising towards the surface. The lake monster's beaver tail undulates underneath them, creates an upward flow, helps them along.

Tara surfaces first. Athena just after. Canoe parts float off in the distance. The food barrel bobs among the waves. The bright orange pack with the sleeping bags and tent inside rises and falls.

~

Pre-Cambrian rocks, the oldest rocks on the planet, wait in a circle in the bottom of the lake.

Sean holds his breath as he falls. He holds on, too, to a story of Tara's hand reaching his, of Athena's body swimming close enough he can grab her harness and she can pull him to the surface. He calls without words.

Tara. Tara. Athena. Athena.

~

Sean remembers the day they picked Athena up from a farm in Saskatchewan, took her from her mother and her siblings, the kind family who cared for her, the only family she'd known.

Athena sat on Tara's lap in the passenger seat while Sean drove with one hand resting on the puppy's soft black fur and the other on the steering wheel.

"We love you, Athena. We're going to take care of you," Tara said, laying her hand on top of Sean's. He startled at the current of electricity through his skin. "We love you, Athena. We're going to take care of you."

They arrived home after midnight. Sean pulled out the sleeping bags and pillows and lay down with Tara on the living room floor while Athena walked, leapt, stumbled, and wriggled over them, through her new world. She licked both their faces, and they laughed and giggled. More. More. More.

"She's kissing us. She loves us." Tara's smile was euphoria, the best drug Sean had ever done.

I did this. I said yes to Tara. I said yes to Athena.

When Athena falls asleep between them, her nose in the space between their faces, Sean lifts himself up on one elbow and stretches over her to kiss Tara.

"I love you," she says.

"I feel it." He surprises himself with his honesty. He is close to saying: *I love you, too.* The electricity feeling grows and grows.

Soon, Tara is asleep, too, but he stays up, watches his girls fall asleep. He rests his hand half on Athena, half on Tara. Each breath deepens the current inside him, each moment lengthens with peace. His sleep, when it comes, is glorious.

His memory releases him. He lets go.

His falling stops. His floating begins.

~

Tara bobs in her life jacket. She leans forward, tries to see into the water, but she is light and the floatation in her jacket is strong. She's holding onto the floating canoe pack with one hand, Athena with the other. They scan the horizon. No lake monster.

She needs to focus. Let fear pass through.

She breathes in deep and lets out a long exhale. Three times. Her legs relax. Her feet dangle. Then, she feels the pull, a gentle tug, the calling of the Pre-Cambrian Rocks. She breathes slow and steady. The wind dies down. The sun comes out.

Sean isn't floating. He isn't waving from the water or the shore. Athena swims wide circles around Tara, plunges her head into the water, comes up for a breath, swims circles again.

So much is uncertain, but in the light, now, and with the wind gone, so much seems possible, too.

How much time do you have before you die?

Tara unzips her life jacket and begins to sink. She spreads her arms in wide circles. Kicks slowly.

You cannot save anyone.

The one thing she learned in swimming lessons, the one thing she did better and longer than any other student was treading water.

You must honour every being.

"Athena, I'm going to find Sean."

Tara attaches her life jacket to the canoe pack.

She dives down to find Sean.

~

Sean's body floats in between the surface and the bottom of the lake. He perceives shadows above and darkness below his body, though his chin touches his chest. His limbs hang limp. His feet and hands and lips buzz; all of the cells vibrate against each other with the last of his breath.

It's pleasant at first, knowing what he knows, feeling what he feels and, then, beautiful. He has mattered. He has been matter.

Sean! Sean!

He hears Tara's voice.

He has a choice. He can see his jelly-fish hanging body. What strong arms and legs. What incredible definition in his jaw. He laughs. What a great head of hair. He remembers his adopted mother. How she loved his hair. How she loved him. He found nature after her death. He found Tara after nature. And, now, finally, he's found himself. How much he's missed.

How much he didn't realize. Incredible Tara. Look at her. Who she is. Who she might become. Look at her. A fierce searching face.

He feels love. Now, all of her love. And, his.

He can go back. He can call out to her. He's been so lucky.

His whole life has happened for this one moment. A monster, transformed. No fear.

Thank you, Tara. Thank you.

He feels the last of his cells vibrate, the particles of who he has been begin to merge with the water, sink down towards the ancient ones, the rocks below. His body begins to float up.

~

Athena finds Sean's body first. Tara helps swim him to shore.

Back home, grief overtakes their lives. Athena sleeps next to Tara, her front paws hugging her and her licking tongue kissing her when she wakes from a nightmare of a lake monster. During the day, Tara draws moose/trout/beaver figures on scraps of paper. She writes letters to Sean, asks for his help to know what to do now.

She begins to remember his laughter more vividly. Her drawings of lake monsters become popular among her friends. She creates a mural of a moose/trout/beaver on her garage door. A local magazine wants to profile her as an artist. Not long after, she takes Athena to a big lake. They rent a canoe and paddle out on a sunny day. They play.

They go out again the next week and the next, until one summer they paddle for weeks at a time in the wilderness through storm and sun, in honour of the direct experience of being alive.

*Mar'ce Merrell is a writer. She is also a canoeist. Neither beginner nor expert, she survives long trips in the wilderness. She relies on her paddling partner when she's distracted by falling in love with the outside world. She jumped into Ghost Lake on Thanksgiving Day and swam to the shore. Her son challenged the whole family. Everyone agreed.*

## EXERCISES, CHAPTER ONE

1. Surrender. "Water Calls, Water Holds" is paired with the artwork *Surrender* by Helena Hadala. In the story, Tara faces her fears and transforms. Be like Tara, face your fears. Challenge yourself by deliberately surrendering yourself into an uncomfortable situation, while remaining calm, controlled, quiet, focused, and confident. Start with two minutes then increase time as preferred. It can be any situation no matter how seemingly trivial or small. It can even be in the format of visualization. Enter with the ultimate power of protection to learn through dedication and discipline. Always choose a safe situation.

2. Mortality. The story reflects on life, death, and universal human experience of mortality. Tara finds a way to honour Sean's memory by remembering his laugh. Have you lost someone you wish to honour? Can you remember their laugh? What other memory or gift did they give that you cherish?

3. Gateways. A spiritual gateway is a way to access an enlightened sense of meaning, purpose, and connection. The author acknowledges a sacred space of life before birth, 'tucked in a mother's womb, feeling the mother's heartbeat,' albeit through an imagined experience of her canine companion. Do you hold a view of life before birth as a sacred gateway? How might it hold a special connection to the divine or higher consciousness?

*For further study:*

Chödrön, Pema. *How We Live Is How We Die.* Shambhala Publications, 2022.

Blackie, Sharon. *Foxfire, Wolfskin and Other Stories of Shapeshifting Women.* September Publishing, 2019.

## TWO

# SPIRITS OF THE DEPARTED

*Antoine Mountain*

## FOR HIS *SAH BAH SHO*

*Times like this, always feel like a mist*

At times like this, the old Dene granny had to really watch what she was doing. Sharp skinning knife in hand, she busied herself before the real cold set in. She sat to the late fall fleshing the heavy, dark brown, almost black, beaver hide her man brought in.

Tired from being close to the cold water he lay, resting in back of their bush tent, sound asleep, making low, growling noises now and again, her hungry animal and protector.

She was practically sitting right outside on her entrance log. The wall tent kept the inside warm and cozy, but here only a thin blue tarp on supporting poles kept the winds from breezing right on in. Though she could plainly see frost on the poles, its plastic did help to reflect some good heat.

Agnes's real company was the wood stove right behind her, almost touching, throwing its steady spruce heat into her aching back. She never complained about it, but all the wood hauling just like a man, before she was married, made that part of her ache, even in rest.

In its way, this was the best part of her day, alone, the grandchildren just out of muffled earshot, out there in the trees somewhere, probably chasing squirrels.

The more of this bush tea she drank, a mix of brittle *ledi mahgih,* Labrador tea, and Red Rose, the more it brought back memories of a lost daughter, Yah Sileh. When just a teen she was lost to them, to these high country streams they always returned to.

"Even a dream is better than nothing," the old man always grumpily said. But leaving it at that was not enough for the aging matriarch. Sometimes the rest of their clan came along, but lately more to just help set up camp and leave some of the dogs for protection. There were any number of bears still roaming around for a good last bite of fish or whatever else left unattended.

The days were getting shorter, in a few months to only a few hours to do all of the day's work. This world then turned to all black and white. Now ol' Agnes's uncertain thoughts turned to her own mother and grandmother. She had seen them countless times, doing exactly as she now did and showing her all the parts she really had to watch out for, to get the darkest of hides from what she got.

"I want his busy hands, even tired, to do all the things needing doing around here. Wood has to be cut for every day we are here, for the entire winter this time."

She thought of the way he got up so early she hadn't even settled down to her sewing yet. The only sign of her man having been there was a half-empty tin cup of his strong tea. He even liked it cold, too, like the coming winters.

"All this really brings him to life, and here I am feeling so sad!"

Over the hours she now spent simply working steadily towards his *sah bah sho*, winter beaver mitts, the old Dene woman found herself kind of caught between the generations.

True, her granddaughter would pick up these skills, in a few years, which was heartening. For now, the two youngsters came back to warm their hands by the fire and have some frozen bannock and a sip of her tea.

As an Elder, Agnes was set in her ways and liked to just keep to the basics. Another knife stood ready, stuck right into the wood.

This she thought of her anger over her daughter's untimely passing. An old lard-can spittoon caught whatever snuff she was fond of chewing, spitting out some unpleasant thoughts, now crowding in. On the far end of her log her favoured small axe, wedged, for use later, for the stretching frame.

"I'll have to ask the old man to do that when he gets up," she nodded. "But better take the axe in first, warm it up."

Brusque though her manner, the aging woman had been taught to keep her 'visitors' in mind. Spirits of the past and those 'other' presences always around these favoured of Place, found ways to make themselves felt, known. These ancestors wanted to make sure this was a camp with no idlers, ones who kept them in mind by tidying around.

This one now, was not far, practically to foot. Yah Sileh, her lost daughter's insistent self, first as fresh-fallen snow, then attached to camp support poles ... ever nearing ... even resting.

Now back to the last of this fleshing, Agnes moodily thought, Even though you try your best, Life has its way of cutting you short, taking something else away, leaving you like this. Yah Sileh would've been right here, sitting beside me on this entrance log, joking about who knows what!

Then again, there's these mitts to do. That old man is getting on in years, like me, but we still have to think ahead, what we need." With that she reached for her tea, putting her knife, file, hide and her petty worries away, to stretch later, on its sapling spruce beaver hide frame.

If a bear can do it, wander off with a full stomach
and just sleep this weather away,
so can I let the freezing mists put 'em
away someplace safe.

*Soon I'll be to the fun part,* she thought. *Put some colours around the trim, fringes, and a long-woven yarn strings. Better use the brightest colours, so he won't lose 'em in the snow.*

## BETTER WITH A KISS

Each time we descend to a new low, someone comes along, one way or another, to make it all better with a kiss.

In the wind, as time, passing, sometimes at rest, healing …
Yet, looking back, as a hunter will, for future use,
it stays with you,
this imprinted dream.
Marked as beginning, in high mountain stream.
Water sprites, tricksters in our borrowed hats,
Rooted to such folly,
Tied, 'tween grinned purpose.

Pools along the way, feelings, lasting memories. Even those deepest, devastation then, with time and Life, defined of face, go to misting,

Joining
The Holy Ones.

This, to truly mark any sojourn, its presence awakened. Others, even to the smallest of brooks, to the tea in your hands, of song and calm relate.

As you sit to ponder, the tale goes on, this moving spectacle, gathered of such depths.

Yearning,
Slowly ebbing on …
To Mother Ocean.
Ever mindful
To Thee
Growing,
… for these stories
In the telling.

# HIS SHIELD

LIKE A SKITTISH PONY in her father's herd, Autumn Leaf found herself jumping at every strange sound. *Gone are the days,* she thought, *when the world I knew was as solid as the ones before.*

Now on a high hill a little removed from her People's camp, she felt the weight of the war shield she carried, a wayward autumn breeze catching at its rounded shape, swinging it away from her tattered dress.

The dishevelled way her blowing hair kind of matted in patches told of her present state, that of mourning, crying for a lost someone.

Her man, Green Tree, was one of the more outstanding of the tribe's warriors, having earned every white tail feather now fluttering along the edges of the shield. In his honour, she carried it along on her daily wanderings in the late-fall hills, hoping for a sign from his departed Spirit for what to do with it.

Of course, she so wanted to keep it, or at least hand it off to someone new, but this was what her Uncle Bear Doctor instructed her to do: find some high-up place, quiet, for it to put at rest her departed man's Spirit.

As men would, little more was ever said about the shield itself, although it was certainly central to her man's life. So high was its value that two fine ponies were exchanged to the Pipe Carrier, who fashioned it from the tough buffalo hump hide passed along to him.

Yet she gladly accepted these duties, even wandering aimlessly alone in high country, where any enemy might spot her. *There is enough reckless bravery to go around amongst the warriors,* she thought, as her endless search continued. The irritating scratch of thistles and thorns on her legs reminded her of this present ordeal. The implement of war moved in her firm grip as a penitent but, yet, wayward son, seeming, yes, to set her free of his memory, but bonded to habit.

*Things must be looking up too,* she thought, for every once in a while, she would catch the distinct drift of scent from Sweetgrass, even here in the sandy highlands.

Her grandmother had told her that Mother Earth had her ways of reaching out from the Great Mystery to reassure her children in moments of doubt. Autumn Leaf really needed these reminders to somehow return her to the Circle. These last days of late summer felt as if she was already aged beyond her late twenties, like one of those elderlies who can't seem to know what to do, nor even where they are. Even a close relative got the blank look.

Just now, she really had to reach to remember the melodic flute tunes he would play for her, way back when they were both newly in love's playful hold.

Too, she hoped for even
a bit of female rain,
… a light water shawl
waiting for the sun

These parched hills felt as she did—all out of play.

She longed for the days her grandmother fondly recalled when as a young girl, she would just run and romp through fields of spring flowers, shouting and singing for joy!

Now her People wandered, as she now did, these foreign hills south of their northern home.

More, Autumn Leaf could better relate to the great but old stump she came upon—it once threw a majestic shade for all who sought its cooling comfort.

Just needing a bit of rest, she lazily flopped into its tired arms …

Distant mountain peaks reached out
Beyond the miles it would take
To Know them

Now at least comforted by smaller memories, she recalled how her man would sometimes toss and turn in their night robes, even mumbling incoherently about a lightning-struck tree…

Could this omen have somehow led to his untimely death?

With Shield now rested between her and Tree, she could feel a growing hum in the small of her back, in a way so much like Drum, sounding in His memory—drumming the coming storm…

Now starting—faint rumblings,
like a deep Voice.
Thunder slowly, insistent,
made its way through valleys…
Of this, her tree
Catching its echo

Passed through aching ribs, to a waiting heart, into Voice, Autumn Leaf now hummed…

*His* Shield, she thought,
not only keeps, but sings,
Of things past,
yes,
But, too, to Be…

As if in answer, the winds from afar brought the light mists Autumn Leaf craved, even as a salve for her aches.

Now weary of bone, yet light in heart, she carefully placed the shield in the sheltered hold of the ancient stump, along with some mountain tobacco, gratefully turning to the arms of village and family hearth.

Too, the distinct sound near her light-footed pace, a sharp snap. Now fully out of the months-long mourning reverie, this reminded her of the turtles she had heard of, to the North and West, and the thought:

This Land, so powerful it has now
Loosed its hold on me …
Playful minnows of mist
Mingled with newer Life within

*Antoine Mountain is from the Radelie Koe/Fort Good Hope area of the Dene Nation in Northwest Territories. He is a Dene artist, painter, and activist who focuses on depicting the Dene way of life, his love for the land, and the spiritualism of his faith. He is the author of* From Bear Rock Mountain : The Life and Times of a Dene Residential School Survivor *and* Child of Morning Star: Embers of an Ancient Dawn.

## EXERCISES, CHAPTER TWO

1. Passage. "Spirits of the Departed" stories are paired with the artwork *Passage* by Helena Hadala. Throughout life, there is a continual passage or 'evolvement'; ongoing growth, progress, and transformation over time. This implies change and attainment of knowledge through choices that come with free will. Have faith in your decided passage and free will. It requires open-mindedness and respect for others' beliefs and practices, even those that are new to us. Within Antoine's Dene Nation stories what are some traditions or beliefs that you are interested in discovering more about?

2. Drumming. Explore rhythms and timings of drumming, even if it is two pieces of wood or wooden spoons on another piece of wood. Keep the body quiet except the hands and arms. Focus on the striking material. Do not think of anything. This can gently or assertively allow you to release emotions and express yourself in a nonverbal way.

3. Resting, Healing. In the wind, as time passes, sometimes at rest, healing . . . . Sit still in nature as time passes, with eyes closed, listen. Then stand and be still—look and listen as time passes, with your focus resting on a different thing each time. This might be an animal, a plant, or a mountain, or an insect. Stand or sit and be still with a loved one, or loved animal, with closed eyes, then open your eyes. Listen, look, rest, and heal. Combine methods two minutes, once each day.

*For further study:*

Storm, Hyemeyohsts. *Seven Arrows.* Harper Perennial, 1991.

Matthiessen, Peter. *In the Spirit of Crazy Horse.* Penguin Books, 1992.

THREE

# NENET'S BROKEN HEART AND HOW IT WAS HEALED

*Islene Runningdeer*

A PRAYER FOR SAMHAIN

*I pray with my grief, with my sorrow, with my heart shattered open into a million fragments, as if the first primordial burst of creation is still reverberating inside.*

*—Seren Swannesha Bertrand*

IT IS THE MIDDLE OF THE NIGHT. Nenet is asleep having fitful dreams, when the messenger raps heavily on the door. "Nenet, Nenet, wake up! Hanon's baby is coming. The women are gathering. We must hurry!"

She knows she must move and respond, but her body is sluggish. She forces herself to come to consciousness. It is her job, and life goes on.

It is 1990 BCE, Dendera, Egypt. Nenet is 23 years old, a Shemayet Musician Healer and Singer. She and her swnw physician father care for the sick, and pregnant, and dying in their community. She loves her work, singing and praying at the bedsides of her beloved neighbours and others. But for weeks now, her heart has not been in it.

Her heart is somewhere else, hiding in a dark cave, full of heavy grief with the recent death of her Ama, the grandmother who raised her—the dear woman who had stepped in closer, after Nenet's mother died in childbirth, when Nenet was but a small child. Ama filled her heart with so much love, so much strength; her mind with so much knowledge. And now, Nenet's heart, her centre, feels empty and heavy beyond repair.

Nenet's ministrations to the sick are weaker now, without fervent colour and power, as they once were. She has lost her desire to eat, walks about as though in a dream, no longer senses the beautiful things around her which used to give her pleasure. At the bedsides of her patients, she loses her concentration, struggles to breathe and sing, even trembles while she shakes the sistrum. "What am I to do?" She worries and wonders. "I feel as if I've died with Ama. Oh, goddesses of life and health and strength, please send help. I am in despair."

In a dark cloud of sorrow, she rises, dons her warmest linen cloak and sandals, and heads out into the chilly night with her sistrum and harp to do her duty. The way is as dark as her own heaviness, a sliver of a new crescent moon barely lighting her way. She raises her torch with one arm, carrying her instruments in a satchel made of woven flax with the other, carefully watching her swift footing on the cobbled streets. As she nears Hanon's small house, the light brightens ahead, with oil lamps in all the windows, as all are awake inside and busy helping the young mother bring her child into the world.

Suddenly, like a flash, a creature nearly trips her as it darts across her path, makes a sharp turn and follows her to the doorstep. In her rush to get to Hanon, she barely notices that it is a black cat. She is annoyed by being thrown off balance, but thinks, "Perhaps I will need the spirit of a cat to help me get through this night." As she closes the door behind her, Black Cat sits outside by the threshold, taking the pose of a patient sentinel. The cat is nearly invisible in the dark night. But, there is a shimmering presence about her that glows. She is serene, with eyes alert, as the hours pass. Nothing will make her move from her post.

In her hurry to get to the task at hand, Nenet did not yet realize that special help had just come her way. Nenet's people believe that cats embody the divine spirits of gods and goddesses they revere. They bring practical protection to a household as hunters of dangerous prey, snakes, rats, and scorpions. As well, they offer other protection and aids related to illness, both physical and emotional. She had prayed to the gods for help, and finally it was delivered. The magic of Black Cat had just appeared.

Hours later, just as the sun was rising above the far desert horizon and after Hanon's infant was safely delivered into the world, Nenet packs her instruments and steps out onto the street. Black Cat is still quietly waiting by the threshold and meows in greeting. Tired from the night's work, Nenet nods in her direction and heads home. Black Cat follows her all the way, and it is only then that Nenet gently shoos her away and tells her to go home. "Your keeper must be wondering where you are," she says. Nenet closes the door behind her, drops her cloak and bag to the floor, steps out of her sandals, and sleeps. She dreams of Ama.

Ama appears as her younger, healthy self—the woman Nenet remembers when she was a small child. Her sweet, benevolent smile and outstretched arms express the great love she feels for Nenet. When Ama speaks, it is only in vibrating tones, but somehow the meaning is clear. "Have patience, my child," she conveys, "For help is at your doorstep. I am well in my new soulful state, and you will be well again soon too. I will always and forever be with you, my dear one. Look for the signs."

Nenet wakes the next morning, not quite remembering her dream, but sensing the energy about her has shifted. Black Cat again appears while Nenet is on her healing rounds. "Hello, Black Cat. It's nice to see you again," says Nenet. Once more, the cat follows her to her patient's home and waits steadfastly for Nenet to reappear. She again follows her home, asking to be let in. But

Nenet says, "Go home, Black Cat, someone is waiting for you there."

For three more days, Nenet and this mysterious creature have the same encounter. When Black Cat meows more boldly to be let into Nenet's house, she is finally allowed entrance. It dawns on Nenet that this cat may indeed be an important sign, sent to her from the benevolent goddesses—a friendly companion whose direction she should follow. A foggy memory of Ama telling her to look for the signs crosses her mind.

For that brief moment, she recognizes that perhaps an iota of her power remains, if she is able to see a sign placed in her path. She hopes so. This is the first time since Ama left her that Nenet has hoped for anything.

After cat and woman are well fed and watered, they both head for bed, together. In her loneliness, which often rises in the silence of the night, Nenet gladly allows the cat to snuggle close to her and lay part of her body on her breast. As she is thinking about Ama and how she always kissed her goodnight, Black Cat begins to purr. Loudly. Continuously. Unceasingly. The warm vibration of the animal is so soothing that Nenet soon falls asleep and dreams again of her grandmother. In vibrating tones, Ama assures Nenet, "Let Black Cat soothe your aching heart. My own spirit will abide as the cat's spirit for a time of deep healing. Know that I will be at your side as you sleep each night, with the purring sounds of Black Cat injecting your wounded heart with new love, new strength."

~

And so it went on, the nightly ministrations of Ama, working in tandem with the sounds of Black Cat. Each night, Nenet retired to her simple bed, a wooden frame set low to the ground upon which spanned a reed- and straw-filled mat. As she lowered her head to the headrest, Black Cat gently hopped to her side. As they both settled in for the night, Nenet stretched out on her back. Like a well orchestrated ritual, the cat's paws gently and firmly massaged various points on Nenet's torso, all the while circling to mark a comfortable resting place. The creature then lowered herself, pressing her warm body and soft fur against Nenet's chest, followed by the easy, deliberate, and intoxicating vibrations of a deep purr. Before long, their breathing rhythms matched; cat and woman became one. Healing energy flowed into Nenet's chest cavity and heart: quieting, warming, comforting and strengthening. Eyelids heavy, her body's limbs surrendering heavily and willingly into the mat, her breath's *ritardando*, all led her into a blissful peace. The tone and pitch of Black Cat's purr filled her inner ear, and Nenet opened her mouth releasing her own purring sound. She toned with the cat in unison, they interwove their voices, and then Nenet broke away on her own chant:

*AAA ... EEE ... III ... OOO ... UUU ...*

These are the sacred syllables of power. Black Cat maintains her purring drone, supporting the rising and falling of Nenet's sweet voice. Neither cat nor woman is aware of this happening, their consciousnesses floating through sleep. Healing occurs. Each night, for many, many nights, this ritual of deep healing is reenacted.

~

For twelve moons, Black Cat and the spirit of Ama follow Nenet as she goes about her days. The citizens of Dendera have become accustomed to seeing this Shemayet walking the streets, closely followed by a sleek Black Cat never more than a footfall away. Wherever Cat is sitting sentinel at a front door, passersby know that Nenet is inside ministering to someone who needs her special help. Father swnw enjoys having the cat on their rounds, and then later on at home, realizing that she provides companionship for a beloved daughter who has suffered a great loss. Nenet's nightly chant, as the household sleeps, is lovely beyond description. He also sees that Nenet seems to be coming out of her despair, is engaging more with her younger sister, sometimes even playing with her and laughing. He is so relieved.

As they work together with patients, he smiles as Nenet's clear strong voice inserts itself more and more into their ministrations. And of course he sees it in the improving spirits and bodies of those who receive her blessed music and sound. The goddesses have surely answered his prayers for help, he thinks. Little does he know that it is Ama, working through Black Cat's spirit, who has bolstered this miraculous healing for Nenet. That special knowledge is only for Nenet herself, who gives great thanks every day for the return of her powers and the love of her grandmother.

Early one morning, Nenet wakes to the early light and shrill cry of a falcon, perched on the wall just outside her window. Never has the god Horus presented himself so closely to her, and she acknowledges it as a powerful sign. She recalls her many dreams of Ama, and enters a strange state of floating awareness, so clear and radiant she wonders if she has died. She sees Horus vividly opening his wide wings to her, beaming his *wedjat* eye in her direction, the strongest amulet of wellbeing, healing, and protection. It fills her with a tingling energy she has never known. Horus is replaced by a hazy vision of Ama, again smiling with outstretched arms, slowly backing away into a golden aura of light, reassuring her that her love is forever, and she is not to be afraid.

The falcon cry sharply wakens her from this strange and wondrous reverie, and Nenet finds herself lying on her mat, her slim body covered with a fine mist of dewy perspiration. As she slowly recovers her wakeful consciousness, she reaches for Black Cat. She extends her arm further, only to find emptiness. Abruptly, she sits up and sees that Black Cat is no longer with her. "Do not be afraid. I will be with you always," Ama tones within her mind.

Nenet slows her breath, tones her gratitude, and rises. "Oh, my dear friend is gone," she laments. To be sure, she surveys the mud brick house, wanders through the small rooms on the lower floor, then climbs the outer steps to the open roof where she finds only her father and sister, preparing breakfast. "Have you seen Black Cat?" she asks. They shake their heads, and she knows that her beloved spirit friend has finally departed.

As she sits with her family, in preparation for the day of work, her heart is full. She is healed. The morning sun's rays beam down upon her and her loved ones, benevolently showering them with protection and strength. She clearly senses Ama and her own dear mother present, sharing this close moment with the family. And she knows, without a doubt, that Black Cat has travelled on, to bring healing energies to another grieving soul. Thanks be to the gods and goddesses, thanks be to Horus, thanks be to Ama, thanks be to Black Cat.

*Islene Runningdeer is a musician, therapist, educator, and writer. Her work blends her lifelong interest in music of all kinds, psychology, physical health, and spirituality. For more than forty years she has used music as a medicine to teach students about creative freedom and health, to aid and comfort patients and families during the dying process, and to draw people with severe dementia out of their isolation and confusion. She is author of the books* Musical Encounters with Dying: Stories and Lessons *and* The Musician Healer: Transforming Art Into Medicine. *Islene lives in Tunbridge, Vermont with her cat Perrine.*

## EXERCISES, CHAPTER THREE

1. SOUND. "Nenet's Broken Heart" is paired with the artwork *Sound* by Helena Hadala. Sound healing frequencies resonate and harmonize with our bodies. Some frequencies can be heard, while others that are not audible are still present and capable of healing. Try placing water in a Tibetan singing bowl or a crystal wine glass and resonate the vessel to make a sound. Watch as the sound frequency moves the water in smooth, rhythmic waves. Set a goal of positivity or pure love without conditions, and feel those frequencies surround you.

2. THE MOON. The crescent moon lights Nenet's way as she hurries through the streets to the home of the mother giving birth. A New Moon marks a new beginning. A Full Moon marks a completion. This cycle appears in many Wisdom Teachings, including the I Ching and other Taoist writings. As an exercise, look up to the sky and watch the moon phases. Whether or not you live by the sea, know where you are in the changing tides. At the next New Moon, begin something that requires time for completion. Watch how the moon's expanding light energy helps the moon itself grow toward completion.

3. RELAXATION. Connect with an animal companion by laying your hands on a safe cat or dog. For about two minutes, feel their chest and throat. Stay still, don't think, just feel their life and vibration. Keep your hands still and close your eyes.

*For further study:*

Goldman, Jonathan and Andi Goldman. *The Humming Effect.* Healing Arts Press, 2017, Rochester, VT.

McKusick, Eileen Day. *Tuning the Biofield: Healing with Vibrational Sound Therapy.* Healing Arts Press, 2014.

FOUR

# MOTHER SON

*Julian Hobson*

THE LIGHT streams streak; razor lights strike my face. I perceive shapes behind closed eyes as the beautiful star rises up over the horizon and is refracted through the ocean's medium. Gentle warmth caresses my skin. I was unaware that such emotion is possible, but I am made aware. Alone in the peace, but not alone, not lonely.

I feel and hear the creaking of timbers dancing with the waves that gently lap the hull. I keep my eyes closed and breathe slowly and to full capacitance. I time my breath with the natural, creaking phenomena and my senses continue to perceive this cycle. I want this experience to continue; I prefer this reward of silence, save for nature—my immersion in the natural realm where no ego exists.

I continue until I hear the first voices. I open my eyes slowly without moving a muscle in my body, completely still, like a lioness before she pounces. I am alert. I am back with the ego; theirs, mine. The eternal infinite experience is over, for now. It is time to learn. Learning through pain and suffering, finding wisdom and knowledge, and then finding further ways to evolve my self, which is integrated in permanence with my tissue. Every time I close my eyes. I know this, I feel this.

I signal to the bosun. He acknowledges and barks commands to all concerned. It is dawn: we are approaching our objective. England expects that every man do his duty. Duty has been drummed into me ever since I set sail from the other Spice Island, my home, Point, Po'm.P., the gated, walled, densely populated and architecturally crowded space that guards the Harbour of Pompey and Portsea. This is a den of iniquity, inhabited by everything and everyone who ever had a hand in manipulation, chaos, and base survival. The concentrated mass of souls that inhabited purgatory, now in human, material form. The gate to enter Point from the civilian sector could have read on its signage, "Abandon hope all ye who enter here."

I close my eyes and remember everything in a moment, faster than the speed of thought; its expanse is all there for me, instantly. I have learned time is a perception that can be utilized. My memories of my mother who loved me more than words can say. My father who kept us alive, surviving, making sure we could eat and feel safe. I understood even then that his intention, although honourable and loving, could never affect our, my, true path of fate, sorrow, and presence. I was always going to be right here, with my eyes closed, remembering, no matter how strong or well-intentioned he was, or how loving she was. And I can control this moment to receive it all because it is within me.

I have learned aboard this ship that time does not have to be within me; it is truly external to me. Infinity, divinity, eternity, all possibility, all probability and free will are within me, and I can surrender to all of it. They are my river, my power, in essence and in summation they are my divine flow, flowing through me.

I receive all of it up here, alone, every time I come to this crow's nest lookout platform, high on the main mast. Every time I close my eyes, I open my heart and receive. I always choose peace within me. I always choose peace for others within me. I survive to serve myself and others, within me.

I do my duty for England but it is not within me, it is my lesson, so I can perform with light, within myself. My free will is how I guide myself through the divine flow. I make choices that are symbiotic with who I really am. My challenges, my lessons, the rapids, the boulders, the log jams I navigate. But I surrender to the force pushing behind me, I use its power and choose the path delicately with my free will and save much energy.

~

I open my eyes after what appears to be a blink. The bosun calls up to me to change the order of the flags, the 'signals' to read the name of the ship, *HMS Psyche*, and "England expects that every man will do his duty." I do this quickly and efficiently. They trust me, he trusts me. That is why I am up here. I navigated this position wisely. I am low profile.

We are part of the small fleet about to catch the Dutch on the Cape, by surprise. The great principle of war is 'surprise'. Notwithstanding I am not surprised by anything. I see how engaged and intelligent Rear Admiral Popham is; I observe him with neutrality. I surrender to his existence, but dissimilar to his surrender to Lord Horatio Nelson's existence, now, and when he was alive

Only a few months after the national mourning of England's hero and the start of my press-ganged contract, here stands Popham, representing the Empire ready to 'take' and gain honour, award, fame, and fortune. He must survive to gain this, and I know it will be temporary. He may not know, or care. So, yes, intelligent, but wisdom and evolvement is another matter. Like Spice Island, wisdom transcends class, race, gender, culture, religion, nationality, and skin colour.

We are in sight of the enemy, the Dutch. The Cape is also our enemy; we were lucky. We navigate and use the force of sea, and wind, and sun. We are still alive. Whatever happens today, I know I will be and I am loved. It is all within me. I fill myself with love. I surround myself with love. I am with the love. I am ready and I am not afraid.

I do not want to fight. I do not want to kill my enemy or anyone. I know, I understand like any marine, any sailor, any serviceman; they want to go home to love, they want to survive.

Even my enemy thinks like this. But we will fight. We will kill. We may not go home, but we will all return to pure love at some point. I will remain neutral and still fight. I accept my fate and know my actions. It is already decided, my destiny. I am only responsible for my navigation within the true force. I accept. Or maybe I will just stay up here in this crow's nest forever. I can choose because I know there are many options. There are infinite options. With so many options, so many outcomes I am motivated to survive, to guide, to galvanize, to teach, to learn, to love, to heal, and to evolve.

Although I still feel the stars radiating power, this combines with the sensation of cold. Cold from the sea, the air, the timbers, the rope, the sail. Cold rejuvenates, refreshes me, heals me, strengthens me. All of me, my mind, my soul, my body. It checks my ego. It gives me this moment with clarity. It helps me achieve, it assists me and I cooperate with it.

The first salvo is initiated port side from twelve of our twenty-four long-range cannons. My eyes are fully opened. I arrive back to my body fully integrated in every tissue, every fibre, every muscle, every strand of my DNA. Mind, body, and spirit are one. I am ready. I am always ready.

I am to stay up here in the crow's nest in case new signals are required. There is a numbering system for each flag, and I remember the order perfectly without thinking. I get to see a bird's-eye view of the activity, unlike those on deck. I only understand our view, our part; I do not have the Admiral's plan. I do not need it. But still, I have my perspective, as we all do.

I know the Admiral's plan is more complex than the view I have. Our cargo may reach its destination. I hope the spices evoke that sprinkling of magic resonating in delightful stimulation that opens the secret code of the pineal gland, falling into infinite wisdom. Taste me. Taste us. Feel everything.

The Dutch do not have time to respond effectively. I see them scurrying chaotically at the harbour, on their undermanned ships and on the coastal fortifications. Other salvos are simultaneously fired from our sister ships, over the top of our invading marines, covertly inserted overnight. The white-skinned, green-uniformed, fair-haired Dutch soldiers and Indigenous collaborators are no match for our surprise—a well organized, and red invading force. I realize I need a piss. I am not losing control of my body; I just need the head. I am human. I see orange flags fall and then raise in our possession.

My ego kicks in and I feel pride. For a moment, I remember I could have been one of them but engineered and navigated a different path—a path that I thought and felt was best for me. I realize that in this moment, again, I am always going to be right here. The perfect place, the perfect choice, the perfect colour, the perfect evolution. I smile, almost not a smile, but a smile none the less. My body is in alignment once again with peace as my ego is tamed. I return to neutrality and survival.

There is resistance, a small pocket. Below me on our ship I hear the sound of cracking timbers, then the sound of the firing of the cannon that arrives, delayed from a Dutch vessel using its cannonades. They are so close I see the VOC coat of arms overlaid on a blue, red, and white horizontal flag. The mizzenmast is hit; it comes crashing into my mast and I lose control of my piss, and hold onto the broken footing now leaning well out over the water.

Our flagship, The Diadem, to the Dutch rear, opens fire on the Dutch vessel, and the barque quickly jibe turns and runs with its higher velocity. But it doesn't get far before it is disabled. It feels good. We are being protected. We are lucky he likes the spice: we are not supposed to be here. Black Market.

A second barrage of close-range fire hits our hull and releases our cargo to the air. In a jolt, I am with barrels of spices falling to the bottom of the ocean. I am underwater, still in my footings, I see, I hear, I feel, I smell, I taste. I am not alone; I am love. I keep descending into the depths, I feel the pressure increase. I try to pull away from the mast. I am free but still descend like a rock. My negative buoyancy is past the point of return. The small pocket of air now in my lungs is forced out and replaced with cold water. Peace is all around. Warmth, love, support. I am home. I choose my colour. Almost not a choice, but a choice none the less, and I know it will be more than the incredible world. It will be the infinity of divinity. It is.

In this moment, my spirit begins to separate from my body. My spirit to the soul is the aurora borealis to the sun, an envoy, the snowflakes from a cloud. I have the pleasure experiencing the two states of existence, understanding immediately how essential my life is in the human form. I cannot evolve from human form, from the human heart unless my soul feels the human and heart's presence. Therefore I must experience the body. This is my River.

In this peace, a memory emerges of love, and fun, and laughter where the air is filled with the fragrance of nutmeg, clove and mace. The tangy taste and smell of the spices all around me can be seen floating as specks surround my body and I am taken, without time, back to mother on Spice Island. We sit together at home, packaging spices, ready for storage. All fear, trepidation, anxiety is absent.

My senses are only here with my mother. All I feel is love and laughter by the fire in a loving home. Only love matters, love that does not try, it flows with great force but is peaceful and unstoppable, like the change of the tide in the harbour entrance. It is timeless, boundless. I see the specs of spices in the air all around me as I sit with mother. I take in the fragrance with a smile. The love remains and I am calm. I can sense the spices even stronger now. It is beautiful and stifling at the same time.

My integration with the body, my DNA and every molecule that carries my soul to enlighten it, is unique to me in every way, so I can experience this journey perfectly. My first-rate frigate was built to divine bespoke order. It gave me all the energy, all the power, all the sextants I needed to carry me here, exactly here at this time and this place.

I am grateful. I accept. I surrender. I understand it's another piece of my evolution. It's not a step. It's all around me 360 degrees, but it is multi dimensional. How many degrees? 720? 1440? Oh! I see. Infinite degrees. Infinite discs around the sphere. It never stops. Evolution never stops. Divinity is infinite for eternity. Of course! Wait, I already know that. I am being reminded. Evolution is infinite, and I see, that is okay, it is not exhausting, it is exhilarating, it carries on. Energy is never destroyed it is just reformed. That is okay. I am neutral. This is perfect. No ego. Acceptance? Not even that, it is way beyond acceptance. Acceptance would indicate a conditional choice. This is not required. Words do not do this justice. In a speed of presence faster than thought, all understanding and what was explanation exists for perusal, for flow.

~

I am still partially connected to my body; I still feel it in my heart. I view the mast, my body, the trapped barrels of spice that followed me from their storage in the hull, now held down by timbers. Some start to rise from the depths to the surface, slowly at first.

I observe and am aware of everything, including the 794 bodies close to me, lifeless, dressed in Royal Marine red coats, most still holding rifles ready for action. These must have been the reconnaissance regiment that never made it when they attempted landing at midnight. I remember the commotion; it was close to our ship.

I see now their colours, not their uniform, their spheres. Not all, just some; the others must have left already. There are beautiful frequencies all around, full of love. The spheres are assisting, nurturing, guiding, cradling, loving. Unconditional love is everywhere. I feel forgiveness all around for themselves, it is for myself too. It is release, it is letting go, it is surrender, no more restriction or control. I see, I feel! This is forgiveness! This is the key to our evolution. No fear, I am not afraid, they are not afraid. They are love. I am love.

My vessel, my ride, my first-class frigate is fading, my breath is fading. I am aware how precious my life and my body are, in human form. I hope I remember for next time so I can cherish every moment and send love to myself and others unconditionally, because I am aware this is the plan, the divine plan. And our free will, our navigation, is distribution of unconditional love.

I am everything; I am unique and I am the same as all divinity. Words do not do it justice. Logic does not assist in explaining this.

This is peace. No pressure, no expectation, no desire, no need for acknowledgement, no need, no needs. Preference yes. Preference is my uniqueness, my identity.

No pressure.

But I feel pressure. I see a barrel dislodge my trapped foot. I am here. I am here. I still see the colours, the frequencies, but I am here. I feel the cold that refreshes and heals me. I am connected to my DNA.

Three barrels of spice, half full of air, smash into my limp body and pressurize me to their curvature, quickly launching to the surface. There is no time still; it becomes more relative as I reach the surface. I pop out of the surface tension. I am still pressurized to the barrels somehow, and another group of barrels hammer to the bottom of the barrels to which I am attached.

My diaphragm ejects the water from my lungs. Pressure the other way now forces air straight into my lungs. I breathe. It's not an option; it is the force. I close my eyes. Everything is still there, all my experiences. I am the sum total of all of them. I open my eyes. I see, I feel, I hear more than I ever did. I taste, I smell more than I ever did, especially nutmeg. I understand perspective, perception. There must be others like me. There must be others dissimilar to me. There is balance, always.

I am not afraid. I make my choices. I will survive. I will forgive. I will be at peace now and in the future. And I will still learn sometimes through pain and suffering. And I embrace all of it with my whole heart and soul. Infinity.

I hear voices and am pulled onto the deck. I am cared for. I accept. I am at peace. I look down at my chest and I am not injured, I am not disabled. But I see the signal flags from the mast wrapped round me, they had secured me to the barrels in every perfect way. The flags, signals, say "England." It is still outside me, external to me, not within. I feel, I understand, I evolve.

Time is relative, time is here, time is not here.

I retain humility and know that the force of my river finds its mark with perfect accuracy, timing, and power. It does this with discernment and specificity. There is no rush, I am one with it and its perfection shares naturally.

I am with my mother, I dance with my dogs that keep me warm and dream with me. I learn from their infinite wisdom and unconditional love. I feel all unconditional love and I transmit.

I am not alone, we are not alone, we evolve. We can embrace our evolvement with love, without condition. Always connected.

I am here, I am home, the other Spice Island.

*Julian Hobson was born in Sheffield, UK, inheriting and developing the abilities of healing through his grandmother. He lives in the East Kootenays of British Columbia, sharing his time between his profession as a cardiac sonographer, his practice of hypnotherapy, and nature.*

## EXERCISES, CHAPTER FOUR

1. Breathe. "Mother Son" is paired with the artwork *Breathe* by Helena Hadala. Breath is the symbol of life. It starts with an inspiration and ends with an expiration. Every time you link an inspiration with an expiration, consciously remind yourself of your life's journey of accumulating knowledge and evolving, through your choices. You can be aware that there are many paths you can take, and this awareness exists in every breath. Spend two minutes each day concentrating on your breath, eyes closed, with an intention in mind. End your session eyes open with one big breath from the sunlight or moonlight either in your mind or safely looking up.

2. Fragrance. In this story, spices evoke a sprinkling of magic, resulting in delightful stimulation. He says, 'I open my eyes. I see, I feel, I hear more than I ever did. I taste, I smell more than I ever did, especially nutmeg.' Do you have spices in your cupboard? Possibly nutmeg, clove, or mace? Smelling spice or essential oil fragrance can enhance your awareness and make life feel more vivid. Enjoy the scents in your spice rack, light an incense stick, or indulge in sample sniffs at the essential oil display at the supermarket—take a fragrance holiday.

3. Connection. We can embrace our life with love, without condition. Always connected. By expressing gratitude to others, you can strengthen connectivity and create a positive feedback loop of kind and generous actions.

*For further study:*

Singer, Michael A. *The Untethered Soul: The Journey Beyond Yourself.* New Harbinger Publications, 2007.

Newton, Michael. *Journey of Souls: Case Studies of Life Between Lives.* Llewellyn Publications, 1994.

FIVE

# THE VEIL

*Kayla Lappin*

A FLASH OF RAINBOW shot out across the reflection of the water as Kate knelt to reel in her catch. The strong trout struggled against the tension of the line.

"Don't worry buddy, I'm not keeping you." Its eyes met with Kate's, if only for a moment to say, "please," and Kate gently removed the hook out of the lip of the trout and gently set its body in the shallow of the river so it could swim free once again.

The last breath of summer murmured through the cottonwood trees that lined the smooth lull of the Jefferson River. Bursts of yellow and orange dotted the bottomland and the air was turning cooler. Fishing during the evening brought a glow of purple curtains on the Tobacco Root Mountains near Twin Bridges, and the first visitations of stars, especially at this hole, which her family called "The Jungle." Being here allowed Kate to set her thoughts straight with the world.

As she looked out at the crystalline surface, her heart glanced back at a time in her life when things felt simpler. If she listened closely enough, she would recall that little girl dressed up in an oversized sweatshirt, throwing rocks from the banks or turning over stones to look for stoneflies that would dart out and into the open water.

She could hear the sloshing of her grandfather's rubber waders in the stream as he came in from his last cast. Kate closed her eyes for a moment to bring herself into a memory that hung like pins in her chest. In the vision, her brother was about ten and she and her little sister were no more than seven. The worm castle they had made in the mud smelled of the algae that bloomed in late summer. The plastic Little Hugs drinks were covered in muddy hand prints as she and her sister explored the vastness of the riverbed.

Grandpa loved to be in the 'in between' place as he called it; the time after the sun fell behind the mountains, before the warm summer day gave way to the coolness of the river at night. Evenings in the 'in between', he'd take Kate, her sister Mary and the other grandkids over to the garage to select tools for adventure: dusty flies in boxes, the cheapest fly poles one could buy, and the reassuring feel of the coolers, packed with snacks. They'd all load up in the old Toyota Tacoma and sit on the tailgate as grandpa slowly crawled the truck over to the riverbed, a half mile away. Then came the approach of the Jungle, a thick place you couldn't drive through, and they'd hike through, looking over their backs for mountain lions that weren't actually there, or maybe a wolverine, like that one grandpa said he saw that one time.

"Wolverines are fierce and can attack at any moment," grandpa had said. The thrill of the wildlife and the pull of the water always meant time for exploring and finding one's place. It was an unspoken rule that you didn't bother grandpa once he was in the water. You could ask him for anything until that moment that his fishing vest was on and the fly rod went behind his back. You also didn't throw rocks in while he was fishing; unless you wanted his voice to boom out over the melody of the rushing water ... or over the rapids either. Don't disrupt the song, don't disrupt the dance.

In this time of quiet and exploration as a kid, Kate began to rely upon the cooler evenings and the slowness as a way to come to understand life. There were few things in life that couldn't be worked out over an hour's worth of evening fishing', she came to understand. And 'fishing', she came to understand, was less about catching than it was about being present to the gift of the moment. The water rushing, the coolness of the water from the confluence of the Big Hole just a few miles upstream. All beating together. All one.

Her throat began to swell at the memories and soft tears flowed down her cheeks.

"I miss him too." Her dad's footsteps made their way behind her. She had lost track of time for a moment. Kate's entire chest felt stretched and heavy. Maybe it was the feel of the change of the seasons, or the Sunday pre-work week blues, or catching a rainbow trout that had to be thrown back, but it seemed Kate could feel the weight of everything in her life building up on her.

"When does this heaviness go away?" Kate burst out. "It's been eight years. Eight years and I feel as lost as I did at 19 when he died. I'm not making a difference with anything. What am I doing with my life, marketing? Marketing is a joke. This whole thing is a joke." She looked up at her dad.

He looked at her while she sobbed. "Come here," he said, and he stretched out his arms. "Earning a living at a job is nothing to be ashamed about. You have a kid, now, that changes things too."

Kate remembered her breath and she inhaled sharply, the 'in between' time at the river was over. "Crap, we'd better get back to the house so I can nurse Lyla." She began to quickly pack up the fishing supplies.

Across the river, a bald eagle circled around and landed softly at the top of a cottonwood tree.

"Look!" her dad whispered excitedly as he pointed at the bird.

Kate looked across the water and up at the swaying cottonwood branches to the talons of a sovereign eagle. Something in Kate paused. And for a moment the eagle's eyes seemed to pierce right through her.

She brought her attention back to the fishing gear which she began to strap onto the front cargo hold of their four-wheeler. "Oh, cool! Gah, Dad, we'd better get back to Lyla." She said, anxiously.

On the way back to the house, as the sun made its final decent and the sky began to twinkle, Kate's mind didn't want to leave the in-between. She heard faintly in her head in her own voice, "What about being graceful with yourself, what about being okay to be right here?"

The pain in her chest lessened as the words sank into her body. The words 'graceful' and 'divine' hung in her mind as she made her way back to the house.

~

Monday morning arrived and Kate lay nervously awake in bed. Mondays felt like she had to hit the ground running. She rolled over in bed, nursed Lyla back to sleep and then as softly and quietly as possible, glided out of bed—not daring to breathe too loudly or move the blanket and wake the 11-month old.

She quickly put on her clothes, which she had set out the night before, grabbed her work bag, and tip-toed out of the room. She began to get bags ready for the day, which always seemed like endless juggle of work and life balance. Each time she washed the parts of her breast pump she felt a ping inside of herself. The guilt of leaving her child in someone else's care ate at her like ants picking over roadkill, gnawing, desperate, ravenous.

Giving birth had propelled Kate into a deep questioning of life, never before communicated to her, a side effect of bringing a soul into the world.

Kate's job didn't offer paid maternity leave, and when Lyla was 9-weeks old she left the familiar rhythm of Kate's ever-present heartbeat for the first time. The separation that formed that day grew inside of Kate's heart like a large fissure in a volcano.

After a while, Lyla woke up and Kate sat down to nurse her before her mom came to watch her for the day. Kate stroked her face as she rocked her in her grandmother's old rocking chair, singing:

*Someday*
*I'll be home,*
*Someday,*
*you'll know,*
*Someday,*
*I won't have to go,*
*Someday,*
*I'll get to hold you*
*all day long.*

As she sang, the inside of Kate's chest stretched and pulled. Much like dangling on the end of a rope over a wide canyon, the bottom of the canyon far below. Guilt shook her all the way down to her feet.

What could be more important than staying home with Lyla during her first years of life? Why hadn't she prepared for this before she had kids? As much as she wanted to, she just couldn't seem to find purpose in her work. She felt like she was in the in-between with her life's purpose.

The sound of tires pulling up in the driveway alerted Kate that her mom, Kristen, was here to watch Lyla for the day. Kate kissed the top of Lyla's head and opened the front door for her mom. Kristen paused for a moment and brushed Kate's hair out of her face, saying, "The mornings do get better, Kate."

"I know, I know." Kate began to rush to grab her bags, wiping tears from her eyes.

"There's much to be said for a mom who provides for her children," Kristen called after Kate, who was busy grabbing bags and her car keys.

"Yeah, but, I bet those moms are doing what they are supposed to be doing with their lives!" Kate fired back, feeling anger rise within herself.

"I don't know about that," Kristen said back, taking Lyla into the kitchen.

Kate's eyes welled up and a lump grew in her throat, but

she stuffed it back down. "Love you so much! See you later," Kate called as she left for work.

Kate turned on the radio and The Eagles' song, "Life in the Fast Lane," was playing on her stereo. Before she shut it off, she realized, there he was, the eagle from the river. But maybe that was just a coincidence.

As Kate made her way into her office and sat down at her desk, she opened her gratitude and dream journal and began to write out ten things she was grateful for, and ten dreams she wanted to manifest in her life. The practice helped her feel like she was moving somewhere, and in her busy mom life, ten minutes was all she could manage.

As she finished writing down her dreams for her life, her coworker, Adler, quietly walked into their shared office. Kate, whose desk was right by the door, looked up and said, "Hey Adler! How was your weekend?"

Adler replied as she walked past Kate to her desk, "Good! We didn't do much. How was yours?"

Kate replied, "Went fishing with my dad out in Silver Star, it was beautiful."

"Oh, nice!" Adler said as she sat behind her desk.

A big fundraiser for the non-profit she worked at was coming up soon. Kate was going over her to-do list for the planning. She rolled her chair out from her desk to check with Adler about a donation from her friend's clothing company.

"Hey did Kory come through with those..." Kate's voice trailed off.

Her mind began to fix on a vision of someone holding an older man's hands. The hands were wrinkled with deep veins with remarkably dark age spots. The hands were frail. Kate felt like the person they belonged to didn't have much time left in the world.

"Oh yeah, I asked Kory last week and he said I can stop by tomorrow and pick up the gift basket, he's also throwing in some coffee mugs." Alder responded from her desk.

"Coffee mugs?" Kate rolled her office chair out into the centre of the room so she could see Adler's desk.

"Yeah." Adler looked up.

Kate stared blankly at Adler.

"For the fundraiser..." Adler answered.

"Right, yes, perfect! That will go well in the auction." Kate said as she rolled her chair back to her desk.

Kate's phone lit up on her desk, with a text from her sister, Mary.

"Buckets." It read.

Kate responded: "Did you hear back from that job application?"

Mary replied: "Nope. It's been three weeks; I don't think I'm getting it."

"Well, just keep at it, you are going to find something." Kate texted back.

Mary sends: "Ahh, thanks. Just hard, I've been trying for months to get a job, and it's getting really hard to have faith right now."

Kate went to respond, but paused. She could feel Mary's heart racing even though she was hundreds of miles away. If only Mary could see what the rest of us see in her, Kate thought. Then words begin to pour out of Kate's fingers and into a text message like water:

> As you move forward into the light and the purpose of your life, the details of life begin to swirl around you. All is felt, all is coming. You are at the dawn, the time before the birds wake up, the time before the stoneflies hatch. Look into your heart and trust that all is coming. Let go of the pain of the unknown and embrace the change that swirls all around. You are not lost; you are not broken. The time has come to see yourself as the one who is moving things forward. You cannot move into the place of security until the water has poured over your hands and spilled from your soul, all must be felt in order to

move forward. All must be allowed to shine forth. Let go of the timing and trust in the journey, you are being taken care of.

Kate continued with a new text,

You must take care to listen to the call within, you must take care to carry the torch of the flame of your heart forward. The tenderness in your heart must be tended, opened, and poured outward. For within you stirs the call. Within you stirs the next steps. Allow yourself to let go, allow yourself to be free. You are making your dream happen, you must trust that with each attempt that passes, you are being brought forward to a place of truth, and a place of harmony with your soul. For as you move forward, you also bring forward your goals and dreams. Do not dwell on the steps, but rather take time to enjoy the journey. Allow yourself to be taken care of.

Kate types, "Holy shit, this is coming from your guides."

Mary responds with a crying emoji and then she sends back, "Gahhhhh. That is exactly what I needed to hear! I literally was thinking about water washing over my heart last night. And had this vision of an eagle lifting me up and into the dawn. "

"Are you freaking serious?!" Kate responds. Her heart is beating fast. The voice that came through was crystal clear. And writing the words felt like such a rush.

"I'm struggling with living with mom and dad, it's hard to allow myself to be taken care of." Mary says.

The voice is back and words again flow out of Kate in a steady stream,

The one who accepts help is the one who is able to give help in the future. By accepting help, you allow an exchange of energy to flow through your parents and to

> yourself. This help is what allows you to give back to the world tenfold in the future. You must learn this lesson of accepting grace so that you may be a beacon of grace for the future."

Mary sends another crying face emoji. "Gahhhhh...again, exactly what I needed to hear."

Kate leaned back in her chair with astonishment. She had never typed up anything like that before. What was once a whisper was now a choir of angels. And the eagle Mary had seen? Really, another eagle? This rush felt like Kate was in alignment with herself for the first time in a long time. What other kind of great wisdom could she access?

She closed her eyes and started a meditation where she only focused on her in and out breaths. As she drifted into the meditation, it was as though she lowered a mask and stood before a great veil. A veil that was the keeper of the physical world and a world of consciousness beyond any human comprehension. The veil was the keeper of the in-between. The place where all life intersects with Spirit. One need only become familiar with the veil to access it.

Kate didn't know it then, but one seemingly small exchange with her sister, was about to shift her entire perception of life. What she had thought was separate before and off limits to her, was actually not.

She pulled herself out of the meditation and texted Mary, "What in the actual F was that?" and a laughing emoji. "That was not from me. Things are literally coming through so clear for me right now."

Mary texted back, "Dude, how cool is this? You're totally connecting with my guides."

"I thought only you could do that," Kate sent back to Mary.

Mary texted, "Well, I journal with my guides and have random souls come to me all the time, but I don't come up with words like that for other people. Kate, I think you need to pay attention to what's happening here."

"Ummm, yeah, I would say so, LOL," Kate typed back.

Too excited to get back to work, Kate decided to go for a brief walk outside of her office.

Kate called back to Adler, "Hey, I'm going to take a quick walk, I'll be back."

Adler got up from her desk, "Ooh, can I join you?"

Before she meant to, Kate automatically responded, "Totally!" Kate was still buzzing with excitement.

Kate and Adler made their way outside towards the walking trail by their office. "Want to go this way, it's about 10 minutes around and then 10 minutes back to the office?" Kate said to Adler.

"Perfect" Adler said.

They started their walk along the trail and pulled their jackets up around themselves. It was cold.

"I'm so glad to have you working here this year. Since you started six months ago, things have been going so well,"Adler said to Kate.

"That means so much to me. Thank you for that." Kate said.

"I'm not ready for it to get this cold out," Adler zipped up her coat.

"Me neither."

They started walking along the trail and near a forest thicket, and Kate felt like she was buzzing from the inside out. Her mind could not stop thinking about the interaction between her and Mary. Had that really happened? She felt a pang of guilt go down to her ankles. She had been walking with Adler for five minutes before she even thought to ask her anything. Kate got along well with Adler and they liked to go running together after work some days.

Feeling like she hadn't been paying attention to Adler on the walk at all, she asked, "So what's going on with Jessie these days."

"Jessie's being Jessie. And I'm being me," Adler responded.

"Mm-hhmmm," Kate nodded, then asked, "How's that working out?"

"It's not" Adler laughed.

"Well, what's your plan?" Kate asked.

"Well he agreed we go to therapy together…"Adler started, but Kate didn't hear the rest of the sentence.

The voice she heard when she was texting her sister was back. And so was the vision of the hands.

"Thank you for taking care of me," Kate heard.

Kate focused in on the hands, they looked like Adler's holding someone else's hands.

Adler was still talking about her husband, Jessie, "I mean I guess it's worth a try, it didn't work last time though…"

Kate interrupted Adler, "I'm sorry. This is going to sound batshit crazy…"

Adler stopped walking and looked directly at Kate, "Huh?"

"Seriously, you can't judge me for this!" Kate paused for what seemed like the longest minute ever.

Adler broke the silence, staring intently at Kate, she could tell Kate was serious, and then she laughed, "Dude, what? Just spit it out."

"Did you used to hold your grandfather's hands?" Kate asked.

Adler was taken aback, "Uhmm?" was all she asked.

Kate swallowed. *Just keep going* she thought.

"Like before he died, did you used to go and sit with him and hold his hands?"

Adler's gaze pierced right into Kate's.

"When he got really sick, I'd go and sit with him and hold his hands at the nursing home."

"And they had age spots on them?" Kate interrupted.

Adler replied, "Uhmm, yeah, they were…"

"On the back of his hands, and he had a gold wedding ring?" Kate fired out.

"Yes." Adler looked intently at Kate with a shocked and puzzled look on her face.

"Okay, again, please don't judge me," Kate said.

"*Dude*!" Adler yelled back, laughing.

Kate went silent and fidgeted back and forth. Her heart swelled up into her throat as if it was on fire. Her hands were full of sweat.

*Can I really say that I think I'm seeing her grandfather? Who am I to say something like this?* She wondered.

The voice came back into her head and whispered, "Yes."

Before she could even think, the words slipped out of her mouth. "He's so thankful that you went to see him every day. And he's showing me how you would hold his hands."

"What do you mean he's showing you?" Adler asked, staring blankly at Kate.

"I can see his hands in my mind, I've been seeing them all morning," Kate nervously whispered back. "There are age spots on the back of them and he wears a simple gold wedding ring. The room is dimly lit, and he doesn't look like he has much time left. I keep hearing him say, 'Thank you, thank you'."

Adler began to sob. "My papa passed away a year ago yesterday. The day before he passed, I sat with him and he would not stop saying thank you to me."

Kate's head and heart began to rush with excitement again. What was that? The trail they were walking on is about to hit the point where they reach the pine trees to turn back.

Adler's tears began to fade.

"You didn't know me last year when my papa was sick," Adler said.

"No, I didn't" Kate responded.

"Dude, you're a witch!" Adler laughed.

Kate laughed nervously, "I about threw up telling you that. I'm over here thinking I'm nuts."

"How did you know he had a gold wedding ring?" Adler asked.

"When I see the hands, he shows me the ring on them" Kate responded.

"Whoa." Adler says.

Kate gets another vision, this time of a pen with the Highland Nursing Home logo on it.

"Was he at Highland Nursing Home?" Kate asked.

"Yes." Said Adler, as her jaw dropped.

Kate's entire body softened into a peaceful trance as more visions, voices, and thoughts poured over her. It was as though she was being shown the entirety of Adler's relationship with her grandfather. The bond they shared. Kate's heart felt full of love and grief. It was as though she was in Adler's body, feeling what it must have been like to love her grandfather and lose him. The veil stood before Kate, completely open, like a mask that had been torn away. A knowing, technicolour feeling came into her heart.

"Thank you" Adler said as she gave Kate a hug. "Things have been so hard with Jessie lately, I am really struggling. And I miss my papa so much. He's been on my mind so heavy the last few days."

Adler and Kate reached the turnaround point on the trail.

"Let's head back to the office," Adler said.

"I'm in shock," Kate said.

"I am too!" Adler said. "I feel so grateful, holy cow, I really needed to hear all of that."

Kate answered, "I mean that was so crazy! I can't believe how clearly I saw all of that."

Adler was looking down at the trail. "You have a gift, dude!"

Adler noticed a piece of trash on the walking trail and bent to pick it up. She turned it over in her hand, "Hey, I thought this was trash, but this is kind of a neat sticker. Do you want it for your water bottle for running?" She turned to Kate, handing it to her.

On the sticker was an American flag with an eagle on it. Kate took the sticker and put it to her heart. The eagle had shown up again.

"Lyla, can you bring me your box of flies?" Kate yelled down to the waterfront.

Six-year-old Lyla was busy picking up stones and catching stoneflies and mayflies underneath the rocks at the banks of the river near the Jungle. The cool spring run-off of water into the Big Hole River was nearing its end, and the Jefferson River would soon drop in flow to provide ranchers with irrigation for the summer haying season. Fly fishing was in its prime, and Lyla was in her first season of fishing.

Kate knelt beside Lyla and helped her put her waders on, zipping them all the way up. "You ready to try your pole out today?" Kate asked.

"Yes, mommy!" Lyla excitedly said.

Kate had taken the day off from seeing clients for spiritual healing sessions to enjoy the summer solstice with a day of fishing at the Jungle. Her dad's footsteps came up behind her and he whispered, "Look over there."

Across the river high up in the cottonwood trees, a bald eagle had softly landed. The branch bent beneath his weight and swayed gently up and down.

"I haven't seen an eagle in ages!" Kate said excitedly.

Kate's eyes met with the eagle's and her heart leapt with excitement.

*Are you ready?* she heard in her head.

*Always,* Kate thought back.

Kate's eyes drifted to the crystal gurgling of the water. She could see mayflies darting side to side against the current. Her gaze fixated on the dance and the rhythm of the stream. She stepped out into the water with Lyla, and as the sound of their waders sloshed in the stream, Kate's mind flashed an image of her grandfather. She smiled gently. The water carried his spirit, as it had also carried her worries, all flowing in and out.

Kate looked over at Lyla and voiced an instruction. "You remember the flick movement to make?"

"Shhh, mommy, we're in the water!" Lyla whispered back to her mom.

Kate chuckled softly and listened closely to the rhythm of the stream. She could feel the veil, the in-between place, and she whispered back to her daughter, "Yes, yes, we are."

*Kayla Lappin is a mom, wife, spiritual medium, spiritual coach, spiritual teacher, Reiki practitioner, yoga teacher, singer, writer, web-designer, environmental communicator, sister, daughter, and the list goes on. Labels aside, she is a Spiritual Medium who is passionate about helping people develop spiritual gifts to impact the world. Kayla lives in Butte, Montana.*

## EXERCISES, CHAPTER FIVE

1. Mask. "The Veil" is paired with the artwork *Mask* by Helena Hadala. Lift up the veil, step out from behind the mask. It is in the way of the light.

2. The Healing Room. Become attuned to your guides and accept their beacons of grace. Accept the presence of a known ancestor in the healing room of light. Fill your heart with love and feel their flow wash over you. This is your unique healing room. Spend two minutes a day here. Become part of the river flow of healing frequencies and energy. Believe in its healing power and appreciate the sincerity and power of love that is transmitted. Enhance effects by increasing preferred time in the room. You can create a unique room by taking it into nature or displaying precious objects. You can also make your visits short, that is, ten seconds or so. Time is of no significance in the healing room, so a short visit is as powerful as a longer visit. Evolve by practicing wherever the you are: at work, home, or social environments (where safe), eyes open or closed.

3. The Subconscious. In "The Veil," messages came as if from a guide or an unconscious force. Automatic writing is a technique that involves allowing your subconscious mind to take control of your writing hand. Decide on a question or topic that you want to explore through your writing and begin writing without consciously thinking about what you are saying. Let your subconscious mind take over.

*For further study:*

Anthony, Mark. *The Afterlife Frequency: The Scientific Proof of Spiritual Contact and How That Awareness Will Change Your Life.* Llewellyn, 2021.

Cameron, Julia. *The Artist's Way: A Spiritual Path to Higher Creativity.* TarcherPerigee, 2002.

SIX

# KICK. STEP. KICK. STEP. KICK. STEP

## *John Heerema*

*Kick. Step. Kick. Step. Kick. Step.*

That's how you get up a snowy mountain. Kick a step into the hard snow with the toe of your boot. Then step into the hollow that you just made. Repeat.

It was still pre-dawn, and he was already on the ice. He'd started the climb early. Partly because you start a climb early. Partly because he couldn't sleep anyway. It didn't matter. He didn't plan to sleep again.

*Kick.* He should have been wearing crampons, but safety hadn't been his top priority, so he was kicking steps into the hard snow that lay atop the glacial ice. Having kicked a step into the snow, he took a step up.

*Kick. Step. Kick. Step. Kick. Step.*

He'd parked out of the way. It would take them a few days to find the car, which suited him. The approach was easy to follow under an early rising full moon. After a couple of hours, he was on the lateral moraine: a long ridge of rock over ice, with the ground slowly dropping down below him. Then he was on the ice. The landscape, rising above the black valley floor, was shades of grey fading to black in the clear moonlight. It was the kind of stark beauty that he'd been drawn to for ages. Air, drawn in breath by breath in the still dawn, invigorated his steps.

The climbing wasn't that technically difficult, but he was out of shape, and so he was starting to feel his legs. He was making progress though. Which was more than he could say for his disintegrating life.

It was just him, the ice, and a swirl of regrets now. It would sure be sad not to see his kids again, but he couldn't be much of a dad for them. Not anymore. So, he kept climbing.

*Kick. Step. Kick. Step. Kick. Step.*

There was a rhythm to it, and the rhythm was counting down grains of sand in the hourglass of his life.

And he was breathing that rhythm. Breathe in with each kick. Breathe out with every step. Hypnotic. Kick. Breathe in. Step. Breathe out. A breath of life with every step. Normal size breaths at first, then deeper as the slope steepened. Breathe in with the *Kick*. Breathe out with the *Step*.

The moonlight was melting into the pink light of predawn, and he could see the first hint of colour on the surrounding mountaintops. He'd always loved that first light. The grey shadows of the mountains acquired shape, and gradually, detail. A ridge here. A line of trees there. Ice on top.

As the light became brighter, he saw the first rays of sunlight on the peaks to the West. Golden fire on icy summits. The sky a deep midnight blue, becoming vivid pink over the peaks. There was a day when he would have brought a camera with him to see if he could capture those first rays, and the gradual transformation of the mountain under the torch of dawn. He remembered a particular favourite image, taken at dawn on a day of wonder. But he hadn't touched a camera in ... he forgot.

He switched his headlamp off and almost tossed it down the mountain, since he was done with it. But he couldn't make himself litter, so he stuffed it into a pocket. Memories of other climbs drifted unbidden into his consciousness. Climbs with friends. Solo climbs. Sharing a rope. Tucking into the mountain face for dear life when a climbing partner dislodged ice and snow from above.

And, unexpectedly, lighter memories: getting together with friends after a climb. Friends who didn't have anything to do with *her.* Memories of glasses clinked together in celebration, and of summits shared.

But now he had to pay attention. He was getting to a more technical section, and he had to pay attention to the route. Going off-route meant getting stuck and having to backtrack. Or falling off before he could make the summit. That wouldn't do.

He was starting to focus now. No time for regrets. Even less time for better memories. On route? What's that obstacle? Getting over technical features was getting harder, and he wished for crampons. Fortunately he had at least brought his ice tools, and it was getting steep enough to need them. His rhythm expanded to include the ice tools. Place the tool in his left hand. *Kick* his right foot into the snow. *Step* upward into the new step with his right foot. Place the tool in his right hand. *Kick* a step with the left foot. *Step* into the new step. A breath for every move. Up and Up.

Now his legs were starting to burn. It had been a while since he'd climbed. Turns out that sitting at a desk hadn't helped his cardio. Neither had lying awake at night, wondering how things could have gone differently. But, mind over matter, a step at a time.

He kept going. He was feeling thirsty, but he hadn't brought any water. A bit of snow helped. He knew that it wasn't really possible to hydrate adequately by eating snow, but he just wanted to get to the top. Unexpectedly, he found an energy bar in a pocket, so he ate that and kept going.

*Kick. Step. Kick. Step. Kick. Step.*

The day got warmer and brighter. Some time into the afternoon, he was working his way up a frozen waterfall. The memory came of an old friend who had died on just such a frozen waterfall. His friend had been climbing the Weeping Wall solo when he'd taken a fall. Not enough of a fall to kill him outright, but enough to break his hip. He'd mustered enough strength to drag himself down the approach. He had almost made it to the highway before agony and death caught up with him.

He wondered if he'd go the same way. It didn't seem that attractive. He'd make sure it was quick. Wouldn't he? The thought came to assail him: *perhaps not.*

Hours later, he was getting closer. And, to his surprise, he discovered that he had been enjoying himself. Not enough to dull the pain. Not quite. But it was the first time that he could remember that he'd felt pleasure. The mountains were spectacular, and he'd always loved being high up on a peak.

Coming up the summit ridge, the sun was still warm, but close to the horizon. He'd have a bit of time on the summit to enjoy his last sunset. An easy walk up the summit ridge, and he was there, watching the sun go down.

He'd time the jump with the last rays of the setting sun. He pictured it in his mind. As he flew down, eternity would fly up to meet him. Peace at last.

Or…? His mind was a jumble of conflicting thoughts. The climbing had almost made it a good day. On the hardest parts, it was almost like his life before *her*. Maybe he could adjust to life the way it had been? But he'd already said goodbye to his kids, and he couldn't go through that again. The indecision was killing him. Or perhaps it was saving him. It was hard to tell. But then it really was the last of the sunset, and it was time for action. Time to go through with it.

He took a deep breath, savouring the sunset, and got ready to jump. Should he try a swan dive? Or just jump? Suddenly he realized that he'd failed to plan for the actual jump. Well … he supposed a swan dive would be more definitive. Landing head first would eliminate the risk of accidentally surviving, and it would be an elegant dive. He took another deep breath and visualized the dive. A graceful ark, and a long, long plunge. One. Two…

"It's the perfect ending, don't you think?" It was a woman's voice, nearby. Startled, he spun around to look for the source of the voice, and saw her. She was sitting cross legged atop a little knoll of ice, looking calm and relaxed.

"Excuse me?"

"It's a lovely way to finish everything" she said. "Picture perfect. No more troubles for you. A picture, frozen in time, for everyone you left behind. That's what they'll remember about you. This moment, where you made your final decision. The finishing touch on the masterpiece that was your life."

"Thanks," he said, not knowing what else to say. It sounded like the polite thing to say, but how could there be another climber up here? This was supposed to be a solo climb, not a shared summit. He didn't care to share the end of his life with some stranger. And how had he not noticed another climber?

"Umm … I didn't see you. Did you just get here? Did you come up by yourself? Why are you still up here at sundown?" The words came spilling out. Everything was suddenly wrong. His plans had definitely not included sharing his last moments with a stranger. What the hell was she doing on his summit anyway?

"It's just me" she said. "I like sunsets. I guess you maybe didn't see me."

"Ummm … no. I thought I was alone. Anyway, how do you know why I'm here?"

"Easy," she said. "A man comes up here, stands poised on the very edge, and gets ready for a swan dive. I dive myself, so I know when someone is getting ready for a dive."

"Oh." There didn't seem to be much else to say.

"Don't worry, I'm not here to stop you or anything. Just go ahead with it."

But of course he couldn't. It's just not something you do with a stranger watching. And anyway, how could someone else just suddenly be here with him? And unbidden, the contradictory thought that maybe it would be better to show this stranger that he really could do it. And do it well, damn it.

So he turned around again and faced the void. Took a deep breath.

But the moment of decision had slipped by. He'd have to get himself ready again. Preferably without company. He found himself saying "Umm, aren't you going to freeze up here? Or are you climbing down in the dark?"

"Oh, I was planning to sleep up here," she said. "I brought a sleeping bag and some food."

"Huh? There's no room."

"Not right here—there's a sheltered spot just over there. And it opens toward a great view of the sunrise in the morning." She paused for a long minute, while his thoughts swirled.

"Look," she continued. "I guess that I kind of screwed up your moment. I can just hang out here while you do it. Or I can try to be a bit hospitable. I've got some hot tea and some food. Even a bit of red wine. I could share."

Casual conversation wasn't what he had in mind. Actually, his mind seemed suddenly empty.

After a pause, she added "So why is this the last brush stroke?"

"Brush stroke?"

"Oh, that's just how I look at it. You see, our lives are like a painting. Not so much a flat canvas, but multi-dimensional. We make some of the brush strokes ourselves: every moment of kindness, or of cruelty, or of love, is a brush stroke someplace on the painting of our lives. They are all a bit translucent, so the earlier marks show through. Part of the trick is to make everything balance aesthetically, and to know when it's done. It looked to me like you were painting your last brush stroke."

He stood silent, taking in the sunset, and this impossible woman. After a very long pause, in which the light faded and the chill of night started to drift in, he murmured "Yeah, I was."

After a moment, she offered "Well, why don't you warm up and have a bite to eat? You can still do it at sunrise. The dawn light's even better."

She half supported him, and guided him to a nearby sheltered alcove. "Here, wrap this around yourself. This ledge makes a nice seat. Do you like wine? I'd hate to see you jump on an empty stomach."

As he ate and drank, she added. "All of us paint in the canvasses of the other people in our lives too. You have kids?"

"Yeah. I said goodbye to them this morning while they were sleeping. Better a missing dad than a broken dad."

"You sure?"

"Being a good dad was important to me."

"and ..." she prompted.

"I've done what I can for them. I'm empty now."

"Is all of this because of a woman?" she asked.

"What else?"

"I can see her brush strokes in your life. I can see who you were before, and I can see how you remodeled your soul around her. Then there's this black glaze over top of everything."

"Art critic?"

"I've been called that."

"With that final act, you'd pretty much wrapped up the story of your life. The jump makes for a nice closure. And you can leave it like that. For the people that you left behind, that can be the end of your story. I guess that if I hadn't happened to be here, that would have been a wrap for you. But...we have a few hours before the dawn. What do you want to do with them? I like stories. How about telling me the story of your life?"

He didn't really feel like talking, but he also wanted to be understood. So he did. Brokenly and halting often, he told a story. The age-old story of love found, life blossoming, and growing into joy. The story of loss and grief too much to bear.

"The fact is," he said, "I love life. At least I've always loved living. But grief and loss colour everything. In my mind, I can still love living. But it hurts too much, and I need the pain to stop. This was supposed to end the pain."

"Tell me more," she said. "Start at the beginning. Right at the beginning." And, reluctantly at first, he did. His life as a child. Discovering books. Friendships gained and lost. His first kiss. School, and enjoying intellectual discovery despite school.

And discovering the joy of being in the mountains. Naturally, it was a girl who introduced him to spending time outside. Learning to ski. Learning to climb. And learning to photograph it all.

Eventually, he came to his kids, and his love for them. Seeing them learn new things, and encouraging them as they discovered what kind of people they were going to be.

He couldn't talk about *her*. Not yet.

He tried to ask his impossible companion about herself, but she gently demurred. "We're lovers of art now, looking at your canvas. Let's see what we like. Let's see if it resolves itself."

And so he talked. And in the pauses, she gave him silence.

Eventually he was spent and exhausted.

"Sleep now," she said. "There's room enough in this sleeping bag."

And so it was that he climbed in, fully clothed. She settled in behind him, her arm over him. And as he lay there, her hand on his heart, he felt peaceful energy coming from her, bathing his heart. Gradually, he drifted into a dreamless slumber, more at peace than he ever remembered.

And in the morning, bright sunlight streaming into the world, she was gone. There was a note: "I let you sleep past the dawn. There's food and drink here for a few days. You're welcome to the sleeping bag. You might want to climb the neighbouring peak: you can reach it from the col, and be back here by sunset if you want. Or the next sunset. Or the next. Time will not pass by in the outside world while you are up here."

Leading away was a set of footprints. Bare feet melting the snow. He wondered about that, and tried to remember what she'd been wearing. He couldn't remember.

Shaking his head, he breakfasted, and looked around. Yes, that next peak looked to be achievable. He could be back to finish his life at sunset, and today would be a bonus day added to his life. It looked to be another beautiful day. A day to push his limits in the mountains and to think about angels.

*John Heerema, PhD is an avid outdoors person and photographer who specializes in large canvas prints of the Canadian landscape. He serves as a Director for the Canadian Association of Nordic Ski Instructor and has built harpsichords. His research focuses on developing tools to help musicians improve their performance.*

## EXERCISES, CHAPTER SIX

1. Boundaries. "Kick. Step." is paired with the artwork *Boundaries* by Helena Hadala—a boundary being a dividing line or limit. In this story, the boundary defines a relationship that fractured, became difficult and was seemingly irreparable. But the character was favoured with a miraculous intervention. Have you experienced a miraculous or surprising intervention? What happened next for you?

2. Taking Care. When we are not favoured by a miraculous intervention, we can create our own intervention. We can start by taking care of the simple things, like remembering that our bodies are animal bodies, and that our brains, with all of their concerns and worries, are part of our bodies. So, when we care for our bodies, we are also caring for our emotional self. Exercise and nutrition make a difference to how we think and feel.

3. The Story of Your Life. Sometimes when we feel trapped in a dead end, it's worthwhile to write down the story of our life. And perhaps an alternate ending or two for where your life could be guided to go. Provide lots of details, the kind of details that you could implement in real life.

4. Gratitude. Be grateful, even when you're in pain. This isn't always easy but you may find it helpful when dealing with grief and loss. Express gratitude at the end of each day. If your thoughts are stuck, try moving your whole body someplace different. Really different, maybe a place that holds good memories.

*For further study:*

Butler Bass, Diana. *Grateful: The Transformative Power of Giving Thanks.* HarperOne, 2018.

SEVEN

# MOVING HER POETIC BODY

*Valerie Campbell*

FOR MANY YEARS, she has practiced closing her eyes to move, to embody her arising sensations, allowing her to find an expression of her whole self through movement. Given time and space, she unfolds and worlds unfold.

She closes her eyes. She waits, breaths, listens. Something begins to arise in her. Where will this tiny seed of a sensation lead her? She is quiet. She attends closely, breath by breath to this mystery. What wants to be seen? She follows the small, still-invisible impulse as her inner self slowly makes itself known. Movement comes.

She slips through the portal, flowing with the movement as it grows and changes. She unfurls her inner landscape. This is her moving prayer. Her way in and down, the deep dive. She distills her experience into language and two words come: refuge and source.

She knows how to do this but that doesn't make it easy. Some days, unearthing herself is a tough slog, wading through the heavy mud of mind chatter and distractions. Other days, she is gifted with a slipstream of an ocean current that takes her far out to sea, gaining access to another way of being, unencumbered by the outer layers of physical density.

Her extended, immersive practice connects her to her felt sense. From this, she taps into the lived quality of taking refuge. This deepening leads her to the possibility of finding a direct access to source. On occasion the noun becomes a verb—sourcing. She allows her moving to take her through an opening to realms of spiritual connection and creative expression.

In the 'moving circle' she gives herself time to arrive, to feel into the moment and listen, attune, wait, and stay with all that appears. The practice asks her to follow a sensory score, not unlike a musical or choreographic score that gives creative impulse a form. This sensory score provides an ever-present guiding map to inner territories that, with care and precision, can be heard and felt. There is always something lying in wait. She does not know what has remained, until now, invisible. She enters into this deep unknown, underground of being, with curiosity and there is, astonishingly, never, nothing. In this never, nothing she takes profound solace. She can always turn to and return to the ever-presence of her refuge and source.

~

As the years go by, she teaches and studies the practice. She has experiences of the collective unconscious. When the way is cleared and her portal opens she embodies her inner worlds, and then, miraculously it seems 'the world' does indeed show up. Mythic and archetypal structures of humanity appear in myriad forms and morph into writing, music, art, theatre, and dance.

She discovers the stillness of the mind that meditators routinely access can also be found by moving; moments of clarity and grace are gifts that come, never to be forgotten, living in her cellular memory, a true remembering—corporeal and felt. And this is when she begins to notice that her inner authority is clarifying and strengthening. She now knows herself through sensations and clear seeing and this delicate yet unwavering quality of knowing cannot be shaken. It is always within reach.

Also, and this is vitally important—she is not alone. There are others who journey with her, some with open eyes. Their practice is to witness, to see clearly. No judgement. No interference.

Presence as practice. They follow their experience of seeing, connecting witness to mover through what is being revealed moment by moment.

A voluntary disorientation that occurs when she closes her eyes, opens the potential journey to the creative source point. The invisible becomes visible. Like in the mystic and spiritual traditions of Celtic *Anam Cara*, this 'knowing by not knowing' interrupts her sense of separateness from the divine and reveals her soul life through both motion and emotion. Inner voices and images spontaneously arise, consciousness expands and simultaneously she 'belongs with' herself, the outer witness and the circle. Open and trusting, souls now flow together, seeing and listening with their whole selves, holding each other in the container of embodied presence, potentiality, mystery, and light.

The witness seeks to embody this holy aspiration without the filters of conditioning, judgements, and projections. A worthy and enriching task to undertake. For her, to see without filters is worth a lifetime of practice—the aim—to see with a benevolent gaze, a compassionate gaze.

Now the questions arise:

What is it to see, really? What is it to be seen, really?

And from these questions she ponders the implications and applications for this practice, which makes cultivating clear, sensate experiences its conscious intention. Seeing is more than visual; it is a fully felt and sensory experience that may evolve into a completely different way to view the world and each other. A way also for her to turn her eyes inward, to feel and experience source, and to internalize its abiding and benevolent gaze.

She moves to let all of this settle.

She witnesses to let all of this settle.

Over time, she notices a shifting in her manner of expression and the articulation of her experiences, her ordinary language, slowly turning into poetry. Her poetic body blooms.

She leaves the circle and puts pen to paper …

## At One Point

At one point
There are hills and valleys.
Here my feet find new terrain
Sloping and climbing
I walk the land
Yet sometimes,
I do not move at all.

What is this new landscape?
The floor rises and falls
Under my feet.
The same places have changed.
The same trees are more beautiful.
The same inner story
Has changed its rhythm.
This landscape has a slow flow
To its song.
The river, once rushing, now meanders.
The ordinary, now miraculously luminous.
This is a place to live.
This is the land of *yes*.

## Slow and Soundless

Slow and soundless
but for the sobs.
I see all the movers
close to the ground—
on backs, on sides, on bellies
small, gentle movings,
undulations soft and cautious.

When I return to witnessing,
all the movers are on their feet.
They have risen from the earth
to the upright world.
They have journeyed far yet covered
very little distance.

As a mover, I rest and seek refuge
in the tactile: smoothness of the
back of my hand across my cheek,
the shape of my calf, plush of my pants.
The ground is hard, but I am soft.
I stretch, elongate and curl in on myself.
I am in a cave made of my own structure.
I am warm and settled there yet
I open again and return to the
outside world

I jump, tumble, extend,
take big steps side to side.
I am exhilarating myself.
When I look for stillness,
I fling my arms over my head.
when I look for stillness,
I must move to find it out.

## An Evening Moving

I saw the Great Grey Horned Owl in the tree
    above the labyrinth this morning.
He watched over me the whole time, head swiveling.
Tonight I saw the moon, huge, rise over
    the edge of the ridge.
I am quiet and waiting in the moving.
Everything is a long time coming.
Rocking, rotating, spinning on an axis,
    elbows coming together, bird-like, clipped wings.
Feet together, hands together, inching,
    shuffling along, falling to my knees.
I find another mover.
Come to rest under her leg, feeling this
    weight on me, resting.
Stillness.
The bell rings.

~

## What I Have Lost

How do I find what I don't know I have lost?
Keep looking.
No stone unturned as they say.
How do I recover what I didn't know I ever had?
When did I lose my authority and who got it when I
    left it behind?
Ask that spot in my back.
Let it have its say—
*Finally.*

## Rilke and Juniper Berries

Rilke and juniper berries.
A sumac fading, yet still shimmering in
    its autumnal coat.
Pale Russian leaves, slim and elegant.
"But in them they bore a moist hope,"
    said Wislawa Symborska

A gardener pulls out horsetail, making room
For next year's blooms.
Cultivation with a hand up from nature.
Channeling, shaping.
"It comes through me and I organize it,"
    said P. K. Page

Gardens in their last days of harvest.
A store painted blue.
A circle of cherished faces,
Reading their words of renewal.
"I would not change my state with kings,"
    said William Shakespeare

## A Long Journey

How do you get refugee status?
How far do you have to have walked?
Carrying everything on your back
Before the world will see you and take you in?
Before you can fall at the feet
Of another
And rest
Until your breath returns.

~

## To Belong

I see the robin's nest
I see a huge blue sky
I see a hedge of wild rose

I hear a quail in the bush
I hear the clanging of bowls from the kitchen
I hear the words, "Let the wind in tonight"

I see you rest her foot on your shoulder
I see your belly rise and fall as you sleep on the quilt
I see a smile come across your face

I feel tears roll down my cheek
But are they mine or someone else's who stands above?

I open the window.

It is time to write.

The Listening Mover

Today I am the listening mover
I am an ear
Self as ear is new to me

Today I see you hold back your tears
I open my mouth into a wide O
And sound a long wail

Today the mirror neurons fly
At lightning speed across the room
So fast that only those in on
The secret could have ever
Seen the twinkling flash of light
Out of the corner of their eyes.

Now of course I know that mirror neurons
Don't fly and I have no idea if they actually sparkle
But pay no attention to scientific fact checking,
All I know is that the sound that came up and
out of me is because
I see you.

## Seeing

I am attracted to the mossiness under the cedar—
thick and lush
And gradually I settle.
One by one things come into my awareness—
the long view, the short view.
Suddenly and unexpectedly, an apple tree *appears.*
Is it possible that it was there when I sat down?
Next, I notice the red veins of an impossibly
large maple leaf.
And then…I gasp…..
What????
A bamboo grove right in front of me.
Certainly that wasn't there when I arrived.

I wonder what else I am missing or have missed
in my life on a daily basis.
I think about you sitting in the road when you fell
and the woman who looks at her phone and
doesn't see you.
A pang in my heart.
Oh never let me be so blind or so cruel.
But the odds are that I have been.
After all, the apple tree went unnoticed.

## An Apology

You know the expression, "The apple doesn't fall far
from the tree?"
Well today that was proven false or I found the exception to the rule because I discovered a lone small red apple in the grass far from the tree.
I am astonished.
Of course I take it as a sign.
Today I need to make it up to the apple tree for my sleight from yesterday.
No doubt I need to make amends for other things in my life
But today, apple tree, I will spend some quality time with you.

*Valerie Campbell is an educator, actor, director, and movement specialist. She leads workshops and retreats combining her decades of experience in theatre and transformational modalities. She is an Associate Professor Emerita, Drama from the School of Creative and Performing Arts at the University of Calgary.*

Footnote: Authentic Movement

The Discipline of Authentic Movement is rooted in dance therapy and Jungian Depth Psychology. It brings consciousness to what has remained invisible; aspects of oneself that long to be seen and expressed, embodied, and made visible through the experience of moving from inner promptings in the presence of a witness. The closed-eye consciousness of the mover allows the other senses to become heightened and there is a shift from moving to being moved. The material arising from the unconscious is felt, revealed and seen by both the mover's inner witness and the open-eyed witness. The relationship between witness and mover provides fertile territory for a corporeal exploration of 'self' and 'other'. In cultivating greater capacity and facility to see, specifically in the role of witness, one deepens empathic resonance and the potential for a lived experience of what Carl Jung referred to as, the 'unitive' state of consciousness.

There is another dimension to the practice of Authentic Movement called the speaking practice. Janet Adler, a beloved and renowned teacher, refers to this aspect of the practice as 'the longing of the body into word'. One learns to discern and speak the language of direct experience in the articulation of what has been seen and moved.

The speaking practice then extends organically into a writing practice. In the group the author belongs to, mentored by Judith Koltai, they also move into the out of doors and into witnessing the natural world. It is in these practices that a poetic form gives voice to experiences that need to be extended and given freer rein. What in the moving needed to be moved and seen, now arises in what is called 'writing the poetic body'. The author shares some of these writings with you in the hope that you, the reader, will be able to sense in yourself some of the lived experiences emerging from the practice.

## EXERCISES, CHAPTER SEVEN

1. Flow. "Moving Her Poetic Body" is paired with the artwork *Flow* by Helena Hadala. In an extended description, the artist offers hope and encouragement about using one's inherent ability to flow through life and to just accept what is. In "Moving Her Poetic Body," the author also acknowledges the power of flow: " ... She slips through the portal, flowing with the movement as it grows and changes. She unfurls her inner landscape." Observe again Hadala's artwork *Flow* and exercise your insight about how both the artist's and author's sense of flow is reflected in the art.

2. Dance. Jung's unitive state of consciousness, a sense of harmony and interconnectedness, can be described as a state of bliss or enlightenment. Can you assign a dance, movement, or gesture to express bliss or oneness with the universe? Have you ever been motivated to dance joyously 'like no one else is in the room?' Put on some music you love and try it out.

3. A Seed of Sensation. Close your eyes and breathe with flow. Feel the rhythm, feel the velocity, feel the capacity. Listen. Wait, breathe, and listen. Something may begin to arise. Where will this tiny seed of a sensation lead you? Attend closely, breath by breath to this mystery. What wants to be seen? What movement comes? Feel all this without desire, without expectation.

*For further study:*

Adler, Janet. *Offering from the Conscious Body: The Discipline of Authentic Movement.* Inner Traditions, 2002.

Jung, Carl. *The Archetypes and the Collective Unconscious.* Princeton University Press, 1981.

EIGHT

# SIMULATION AND LOCAL SMOKE TWO STORIES

*James R. Parker*

## SIMULATION

"SIMULATIONS, you see, offer only a snapshot of a system." Ron shone his laser pointer at the screen at the front of the room. "As you can see, each iteration represents a small amount of time both in our sense and in the simulation. However, it also represents a tiny slice of the possible space, and a small number of possible interactions between objects."

Ron shut off his pointer and looked over the audience. His gaze washed over them without focusing or noticing anyone specific. "Of course, if we were really living in a simulation, there may be parts of the universe that are not important enough to simulate in detail. If we can find such places, then we will have evidence of the simulation itself."

He scanned the audience again. "Are there any questions?"

As usual, there was no response. Then, just when Ron was going to say 'thank you', a man in a t-shirt and sporting a ponytail stood. "Dr. Strang. A question."

Ron looked him over quickly and said "Yes. We have the time."

"Dr. Strang, you spoke of places in the universe that, if we were living in a simulation, would not be important enough to render in detail. What would be the characteristics of such places in space? I mean, could the simulation, if designed properly, make it appear as if those places were simply empty and had not much happening? How would we determine that these were key pieces of evidence for the simulation theory?"

"That would depend," Ron replied, "on a number of things. For example, is the Earth itself of singular importance in the model? If so, there would be a correlation with distance from our system and simulation granularity."

"A second question, if I may?" the questioner continued, "What can we infer about the Being conducting the simulation? Perhaps from the perspective of our observations of our Universe?"

Ron paused and looked up, thinking. "Well," he said, "perhaps not much. But it might be reasonable to imagine that this Being's Universe has similar properties to ours in general terms: gravity, for example. Otherwise, not very much."

"Thanks," the man said, and he sat down. There were no more questions. The session chair stood.

"That's the last speaker for this session. Please join us in this room at 3:15 for a discussion of granularity in simulations. In Salon B we will have a session on ways to detect the Universe simulation. There's coffee! Let's thank Dr. Ronald Strang again." The audience applauded lightly and started to clear the room. Ron closed his laptop and gathered his things He didn't want any more coffee.

The man with the ponytail came up to the front and set his small bag on the table near Ron.

"Hi," he said. "I enjoyed your talk."

"I enjoyed giving it," Ron replied. "Where are you from? A University?"

"Probably no place you'd recognize, but I am an academic. I understand that the idea that we are living in a simulation has recently become a popular one. Why do you think that is?"

Ron looked at him curiously. "We have some TV scientists who are promoting this idea. The public likes to see this kind of thing, and sees it as an explanation for things they don't understand. Many of these scientists are atheists seeking to explain a Universe that appears to be designed, and they have an atheist following. Some are just looking to further their careers. Perhaps they want to be the next generation of TV scientists."

"And you?" the man asked.

"I am following the data where it goes. I fear that we can not know the real truth of it, and so I guess I'm just a philosopher at heart." He smiled. "A hobby. My main area of study is plasma physics."

"I see," the man said. "As an amateur philosopher, have you given any thought to how these simulators or designers would differ from what most people would call a God?"

Ron chuckled. "Yes, I have," he said. "The answer I have is 'not by much'."

"Interesting," the man said. "Well, it has been a very pleasant time speaking with you." He turned and strode down the aisle and through the doors before Ron could come up with a sensible way to continue the conversation. That was an odd fellow, Ron thought. The academy was full of them.

It was the coffee break in the afternoon session of the conference, but Ron was always tired after a presentation and he wanted to leave. He went up to his room and took a nap. He slept lightly, and finally woke just after five, just as the conference downstairs was breaking up. He wandered down to the lobby bar thinking to have a drink and see who wanted to go for dinner. He wasn't normally gregarious, but today for some reason he needed company.

~

The bar was packed with conference attendees. They had three bartenders sweating, trying to keep up. There would be other places. He left the hotel and spoke briefly to the doorman: "I want a quiet bar nearby," he said. The man replied and Ron gave him five dollars. Less than the price of a drink.

Left two blocks, right a block, left again. A bar called 'Haven'. As Ron approached, a blue neon sign beckoned, and he stepped down the three concrete stairs into darkness. As his eyes adapted to the dark, he noticed a tall blonde woman at the near end of the bar, who he was pretty sure was a hooker, and at the other end a man with about twenty drinks surrounding him. It was the man with the ponytail from the conference. He was sipping on a tall pink drink through a straw.

Well, what the hell, he thought. Ron moved down the bar to the seat next to the man.

"Is this seat taken," he asked.

The man looked up.

"Dr. Strang, a pleasure. Please sit."

He did.

"Please," the man said, "I have a number of beverages here. Help yourself." He sipped on his straw. "This one is delightful. It is called a 'zombie'. I don't know why."

Ron selected something brown hoping it had rum in it.

"An introduction would be in order," Ron said. "I am Ronald Strang, professor of Physics at the University of Maryland."

"Ah," the man said. "This I know. I am named Aaron. Aaron Todos. How is your drink?"

"I thought it would have rum. It has something else. But it's good, thanks." Ron took another sip.

"So," Aaron said. "What brings you here?"

"Peace and quiet," Ron replied. "The hotel bar was insane."

"So, that gives us a chance to chat," Aaron said. "Your talk was very relevant to my being here. If I may ask, how long have you been thinking about the idea that the Universe is a simulation?"

Ron took another sip. "It has been a thought I've had for many years, but when it became something that scientists were talking about I worked on it more deeply." Ron looked him in the eye. "You?" he asked.

Aaron looked past him. "I've been doing simulations for a long time. I understand the attraction and the methodology." He took another sip. "This is quite good, too," he said. "Anyway, simulations give you information that you can't really get any other way. Mathematics is terrific for some things, but introduce some randomness and it just can't deal. Am I right?"

"Right," Ron agreed.

"So," Aaron continued, "We do simulations to allow for random or, at least non-predictable, events."

"Yes," Ron said. "I know of that from friends I have in the computer science department. My Friend Ralph always tells me that 'simulations are fun'. The unpredictability factor may be why."

"Exactly. They use randomness to simulate complexity. From a distance the two look very much alike. And, of course, one does not need to simulate everything, only the things that may matter toward your goal. You mentioned something like that in your talk, as I recall." Aaron set aside his zombie and selected a green drink to sip on. He continued. "Why do you think someone would simulate the Universe? Surely that would be expensive. What would be the point of it?"

Ron looked thoughtful, but was really assessing the other drinks available on the table. "I have some idea," he said. "May I try one of the other drinks?" He was trying to avoid paying for a drink as long as he could.

Aaron was generous. "By all means, have whatever you want. I selected them from the menu by the order they were listed." Ron chose a glass that looked like whisky and continued.

"I believe." Ron said, "that the simulators are trying to determine an optimal strategy for generating intelligent life in a designed Universe. I don't know why I believe that, except that it's what I might do." He took a sip: bourbon, good enough.

"Optimal? Why?"

"Because the probability of life forming completely at random is quite small. It is true that some people believe we just got lucky. In that case, we are probably alone in the Universe. Some think there are processes we don't know about that increase the likelihood that nucleic acids programmed to create proteins will form naturally. Still others believe that there are an enormous number of universes and life will form spontaneously in some of those, such as it did in ours. And then there is the simulation theory—that this Universe is a simulation. If that's true, then the simulators exist, and the problem of where they came from is still a puzzle. They may be trying to solve it."

Aaron's green drink had been set aside, and he was now sipping something from a martini glass. "That's fascinating, because I have the same thought," he said. Aaron seemed unaffected by the strong drink he had just consumed, and God knows how many before.

Ron continued. "I've been thinking about your comment about the simulation beings being Gods. It makes me uncomfortable to imagine some guy in a basement in another universe controlling the flow of everything here."

Five empty glasses were on the counter. "Any simulation that sophisticated would imply a technology significantly ahead of where you are now. I'd imagine that this would not be available to just anyone. Perhaps by the best intellects available in their race. Consider the power consumption alone."

Aaron gazed into the mirror on the other side of the bar. "What do you know about quantum computing?"

"A bit. There's very little actual validation of it, but I understand the theory."

"If quantum computing were a reality," Aaron continued, "would the computational power be sufficient to create life?"

"Do you mean in a simulation?"

"Yes, of course. If we could use every atom in multiple Universes, could we have enough computational ability to create life, assuming that the initial conditions were random?"

Ron thought about it. He sipped and thought some more. "Depends on how many Universes there are," he said. "An infinite number? Then sure. A million? I don't know. And it all fails if the Universes all possess exactly the same atoms." He felt pretty smart. It was probably the bourbon.

"There are an infinite number of Universes. I know this. But it is not possible to co-opt all atoms for any specific purpose. And it takes more energy to access more atoms. A simulation being done using quantum computing would be limited by the energy available, and that is not infinite."

The drinks were going to Ron's head—he hadn't eaten. "I can see that could be true, although I confess I don't know enough about quantum computing. I'll do some reading." Ron was staring off into space. He was not focused on anything in particular, but a girl at the end of the bar thought he was staring at her, and she smiled and winked at him. Ron aimed his glance back at Aaron, "You know," he continued, "it occurs to me that the designers would also be responsible for not only physics, but also consciousness. And morality and such things."

"That's true now in simulations you know of," Aaron said. "A first person video game is a pretty advanced simulation. In order to 'win' a game, you have to adopt the morality that the game designer built into it. The rules define the moral space."

"I'm part of a panel tomorrow morning on the ethical issues surrounding these kinds of simulations." Aaron continued. "Nine a.m. and I promise it will be interesting." Aaron stood and picked up his bag. "I have to be someplace else. It would be good to see you there."

"I'll do my best," Ron said, thinking '9 a.m.? Really?'. "Thanks for the drinks."

When Aaron left, Ron changed chairs. No sense letting these drinks go to waste.

~

Ron slept until 8:30, took a shower, dressed and was downstairs by 8:50. There was a selection of beverages at the back of the room: cardboard boxes with coffee and hot water, orange and cranberry juice, a suite of soft drinks. Ron selected an industrial style glass mug and filled it with dubious-smelling coffee. He ignored the starchy confections on the plastic tray nearby and walked up the centre aisle between the rows of seats. The room was sparsely occupied, and he had his choice of seats. He took an aisle seat near the back of the room, just in case the session was boring. In that case, he could make a quick exit.

At five minutes past the scheduled start time they were still missing one panel member—ponytail guy. The panelists were gabbing to one another: one was using his laptop. From what Ron could determine from how he was using the keyboard, he was probably playing a game.

Aaron arrived at a trot and quickly found his place on stage. People organized themselves, and the chair introduced everyone.

Aaron was first.

"Folks," he began. "This talk will not be what you expected. First: yes, you are simulated characters within a large simulation. I know this because I am a representation of one of those conducting that simulation, an avatar as you might call it, if you are a computer game player. A simulated person. My mind is one impressed from one of the scientists working on this project."

The small group watching were silent, and seemed to be waiting for a punch line.

"I can, of course, provide evidence of this if you like." He cupped his hands. A galaxy appeared within them. "Some of you will see this as a neat trick, but I assure you this is an image of a real galaxy in real time. I have also arranged for the planet Mercury to disappear. Some observatories should be able to detect this by now." The galaxy disappeared.

A couple of people picked up their cell phones, but most simply watched the performance. A man wearing a blue tie started sending emails furiously.

"This simulation has been executing since this morning. Each microsecond of the simulation in our time, as I experience it, creates six months or so of your Universe. As your system becomes more complex, it takes more time to calculate the changes for each second. So, when your 'Universe' was initialized in what you call the big bang, our computers had much less to do during each iteration than they do now. If we continue too much longer you might start to notice the difference; we certainly will. Each iteration is now taking a lot longer than it did at the time I consumed my last meal. Lunch, you would call it. That point in the simulation would have been, um, about four billion years ago by your measure."

The guy with the blue tie was still typing. "Just about when life began here," he said, without looking up.

Aaron nodded. "Yes. Our software for initiating life is timed to coincide with specific aspects of the model. The number of stars of the right size and type, the amount of water, and so on. Even then we need to give it quite a push. The probability of an entity as complex as even a simple life form is quite small—almost zero. So, we fiddled. This is only the third time that life has taken hold."

"By the way, everyone. Mercury is gone." said blue tie. "Just gone."

Everyone began speaking. More phones came out. People were sticking their heads in the door from outside, trying to find out what the noise was about.

Aaron raised his voice and continued. People did not get completely quiet, but he could at least be heard.

"I am here to tell you that the simulation is nearly complete, and that it will be terminated very soon."

Now there was silence except for blue tie's clicking of keys.

"We have nearly learned what we wanted, and will start a new simulation in a few days. My days, or, I suppose, the simulator's days. Yours will end today, by our reckoning. By yours, a much longer time."

"This is stupid," someone shouted from the front row. "Get out of here and let us continue."

Aaron frowned. "I have another programmed ability that I am allowed to use. I can remove objects from the simulated environment." He pointed to the speaker and some text appeared above his head:

9200019292 7362EA XOBJ: HUMAN 09182
MALE CC 93AA: XX M XYAS983764HGS038S
START 45.09238 END 47.09387 AXIOJISX
INDEX 98273619763927365447 67672379

Aaron spoke again. "Are you certain I am not being honest about this."

The man looked up at the text and thought a moment. "This is a trick. It's unimaginable. Impossible."

The man vanished. So did the text.

"Okay," Aaron said. "Anything else?"

Silence.

"Right. Sorry, but none of this matters in the long term. The simulation will cease shortly. So, what can I tell you that will matter to you?"

Ron raised his hand. "Is there anything we can do to change this?"

"No, I'm sorry to say. I'm not a real person, you understand. I am a copy, a simulation if you like, of my original. I am only as real as you are."

"So why the hell tell us?" someone shouted.

"It's an experiment. The whole simulation is, of course, but we have never told the denizens of a simulation of their fate. I am doing this now, and we will then observe the result. We'll analyze the data over the next while to see if we should do this sooner in the next simulation, or at all."

"That's my presentation." Aaron smiled. "I am sorry it has been disturbing." He stepped down from the stage and walked towards the door as a din of raised voices filled the room behind him. Ron caught up to him.

"Ever had Chinese food?" Ron asked.

"No, not yet. I'd like to try as many things as I can, though."

"Data?" Ron asked again.

"No, not just data. I am as real as you are, as I said. I enjoy these experiences. Do you have a suggestion?"

Ron stopped just outside of the doorway and stared at Aaron. "Is there a point to any of this?"

Aaron smiled. "Existence is what it is. There is no need for anything to exist, it simply does. Are you real? Sure, as much as anything in your Universe, or even the designer's universe. Do you think they don't ask the same questions? What is the point? Are WE being simulated?"

"I do know," he continued, "that pain is as real as anything else. So is suffering, misery, fear. Perhaps our reason to exist is to help."

"What will happen to me? To us?" Ron asked.

"You will cease to exist, I suppose. Me too. You are now a collection of qbits simulating an individual. I guess that will stop. Who knows, though. Perhaps all of those atoms will continue to do their jobs after we stop paying attention to the simulation. Your universe could simply become disconnected."

Ron continued walking to the hotel exit, and he seemed to have reached a revelation. He smiled. "So," he said, "until we find out, let's start with Chinese food. You're buying."

# LOCAL SMOKE

When I woke up, it was not to the light of dawn, but to the odour of burning wood and grass. Looking out the tent flap I could see very little: no stars, no moon, the trees nearby, weeds and grass. The odor was unmistakable, though. It was not the fire I made and extinguished last night, but it was definitely a fire.

I left the tent and looked about. It was pretty normal scenery, if hazy, and the smell of smoke was obvious. A glow in the East signaled dawn in an hour or so, but no actual fire seemed near, and it was true, by my watch, that the sun would rise soon. I went back inside the tent and to sleep.

I awoke again at about 6:00 a.m. Muted yellowish sunlight surrounded the tent, and through the flap I could see grass and trees. It was oddly quiet. I could still smell smoke and could now see a thin veil of it all around. I'd normally start a fire and cook breakfast, but I was curious, perhaps even concerned, about the source of the smoke. It was my habit to avoid bringing electronics on my sojourns into the woods, so I couldn't search the internet or even tune in the radio. My car did have a radio, though, and I jogged the quarter mile down the path to where I had parked. I encountered no woodland creatures, heard nothing but the crunching of twigs and leaves under my feet.

I never lock the car in the woods; I never know when I may have to leap into it for safety, and anyway, how likely is it to get stolen this far from the nearest town? In fact, for the same reason, I leave the keys in the ignition. This time, that had been a mistake. I sat in the driver's seat and turned the key, but it don't turn over. I'd left the car on all night. The battery was a rock. I turned the key off, hoping that there would be some recovery of charge—it worked sometimes, but it may take a while.

I got out of the car and lit a smoke. Yes, I know, people think I'm 'Mr. Natural', what with hiking and camping, whole food, fresh air and all. But I had started smoking when I was 16, and found it devilishly hard to quit. I had done, for as long as a year, but all it took was one cigarette and the addiction was back. I had smoked the most recent 'last' cigarette a few weeks ago, and was up to ten per day now.

I paced and smoked, and wondered what to do next. My options were limited; I couldn't find out what was happening, I couldn't leave in my car even if there was a problem, and I couldn't call for help if I needed it. I may as well try to relax, make breakfast, maybe do some reading. That became my plan.

Still, it was hard to ignore the knowledge that something was on fire. It had been dry for the past month, and it wouldn't take very much for a small fire to become a very large one. As I walked back to my campsite, I pondered ways to escape if I needed to. There was a small river about a half mile south. If I could get there maybe I could float downstream and out of trouble. That is, if the fire was in the right place. If there was a fire nearby at all.

I was thinking mainly about food when I got to the campsite. I started a small fire in the ring of stones I'd set up the night before, and fetched out a can of bacon, some powdered eggs, beans, and some biscuits from my pack. In a few minutes, I had a pretty hearty breakfast going in a pan and had nearly put the fire threat out of my mind. I was immersed in my own smoke.

I was just soaking up the last of the bean sauce with the final biscuit when a warm breeze arose and blew a thicker patch of smoke over the campsite. All at once it was hard to see. I considered running for the car, but as that was the direction from which the smoke was coming, the idea was dismissed quickly.

So, thick smoke to the northwest, impenetrable woods to the northeast, God knew what to the southeast, and the river to the south. Assuming there was a wildfire, I put out my own cooking fire, grabbed my backpack, and scampered down the slope towards the river, slipping on the gravel, grabbing the roots of the dogwood and potentilla to steady myself. Half way down I heard a muted explosion. If that was my car, then there was a fire, and it was quite near.

I reached the bottom and pushed through the brush growing along the shore, or what had been the shore. The river was nearly dry, reduced to a mere trickle that ran down the middle of the rocks that had lined the bed of a waterway that was fifteen feet across, and had been four feet deep when I was here last year. It had been a hot and dry summer, but I had no idea how hot and dry until now. Living in a city removes any perspective of what the real world is doing. I had no investment in rain, or heat, cold, or wind. In my apartment, I was insulated from these elements, and only had an interest in them when I went out to hike or camp. Like now. Weather and floods happened to other people, brown people in equatorial places. Not to me.

Today it was me, though. I looked back and the entire rise behind me was glowing red, backlit by the blazing death of the wood I had so recently slept in. The flames themselves shortly became visible, as the conflagration spread east and west behind me. Half a mile seemed far too near, but that distance shrank as the brush below the ridge was consumed. I really had no place to go. I could not outrun the fire, I knew that. I did the only thing I could: I found the widest spot in what had been the river and sat in the center, near the shallow dribble that remained. I was surrounded by rocks. Who knows, perhaps I could survive.

Within a few minutes, the fire had overflowed into the tiny river valley. All along the northern horizon was a wall of flame and smoke thirty and more feet high, and it was marching towards me. I watched as it leapt the valley to the west and continued its march south, and east towards me. I could feel the heat. The smoke was rising, so it was not a problem, but the heat would soon become an issue.

It is interesting, now that I tell the tale, that the sound was not something I paid attention to. It had initially been silent, but when I reached the river I could hear it crackle and breathe. Trees fell and took friends with them. It got louder until it didn't sound like a fire at all, but like the ocean or a storm. Different but equally powerful elementals.

The fire kept spreading as I sat there, helpless, feeling the heat grow and the fire spread in all directions. I would shortly be surrounded, and, I feared, dry roasted. I had no choices. I had no easy way to kill myself to spare me the suffering I anticipated, and I was certain I didn't have the nerve to take my own life anyway. So, as the fire crept towards me from all sides, I splashed myself with the now warm water from the river and lit a final cigarette.

I inhaled deeply, aware of the irony. Smoke and fire surrounding me, about to kill me, and me enjoying my final Player's Light, also fire and smoke. I tipped my head back and blew the smoke to the sky, to mix with the burned flesh of the trees. I was a little dizzy. Lack of oxygen, I expect, both the cigarette and the oxygen depletion due to the firestorm. I took another drag and exhaled, and that's when things went a bit strange.

First, the sound seemed to fade into a distance. The roaring of the wildfire became a background noise. The wind and the flames seemed to slow down, and I became aware of a dark patch in the flame nearest me. It grew larger, and resolved itself into the figure of a person. A dark-haired man in a grey robe was walking directly towards me. I took another puff. He smiled as he approached. When he was within a few feet of me, he looked down and spoke.

"I see," he said, "you are enjoying my display. You are on fire? Is that pleasurable?"

Who was this? What the hell was he talking about? Ah, the cigarette.

"Uh, no. I mean, I'm not actually on fire. I'm simply enjoying the smoke." I held up the half-smoked Player's.

The man stared down at me. "Human, right? I have never met a human who inhaled smoke and sat in the middle of a fire. It seems odd to me."

I smiled at him. It was probably more of a grimace. "You seem odd to me. You walk out of a raging forest fire and start talking to me." I thought for a moment. "Would you like one?" I displayed my half empty pack of Player's.

The man had no expression, but suddenly responded "Yes, that might be interesting." I passed him the pack, and he pulled one out.

"Do you want a light?," I asked, and then felt immediately foolish.

"No," he said, and put the cigarette into his mouth. The entire thing burst into flame and disappeared into ash.

We were silent for a moment. "That's not exactly how you do it," I said. "May I?" I took out another cigarette and lit it myself before giving it to him.

"When you put it between your lips, gently suck in some of the smoke and inhale it. Don't burn it all at once."

He took the stick from me and did as I suggested.

"Hey, not bad. Much better than the trees and bushes here." He took another drag.

"So," I said. "My name is Mike. I'm pleased to meet you." I watched as the flames around us moved in slow motion. Who was I to argue with an event that seemed to be saving my life? It was very strange, though.

"And you are?"

He exhaled a massive cloud of smoke. "I have been called *Kōjin,* and *Grannus, Mixcoatl,* and *Pele.* Humans have named me *Gerra, Vulcan, Zhurong,* and *Logi.* I think the most accurate understanding of me was by the people who named me *Ra.* They were among the earliest ones, and seemed to understand me best." He took another drag. "You can call me Ra".

"Okay. Ra it is. You know, the Egyptians thought you were a God. Are you?" I had no idea what I was doing, at this point. I just didn't want him to leave, because then I would die.

"These are remarkable," he said. "May I have another? And no, I'm not a God as you would understand it. I am more of what you would call a…cryptid, an alien. Someone from somewhere else with different propensities than you." I gave him another cigarette, and he lit it from his finger.

"Of course," he continued, "from my perspective you are the alien, but never mind." He inhaled deeply.

"Those are supposed to last longer than a minute," I said. "You can smoke them more slowly. It's actually better to savour them."

"Ah, I'll try that. Anyway, I'll be moving on. Interesting speaking with you." He started to walk past me.

"Why not stay and talk?" I asked.

"If I stay here too long I'll run out of combustibles. I have to keep moving when on the surface."

"What? You aren't on fire."

He looked at me as if he were a bit confused. "I am the fire. Everything you see around you, that's me. This package you are speaking with is a construction, a nice one, but delicate."

"Can I walk with you a while?" I asked.

"I guess so. You will share your delightful tubes, and we can talk a bit. It's been a long time since I did that."

I gathered my backpack and we both set off to the south at a good pace. I was sweating like a basement water pipe, but there was no way I was going to lose contact with Ra. He smoked; we talked. He was born in a star, apparently, which one he was not certain. He could stay for long periods in relatively cold temperatures but was powerless in that state, sometimes hibernating. Heat was his element. Fire, electricity, fission, and fusion.

There were others like him. Not here on Earth, but elsewhere. Not all were as friendly as Ra. He did not start fires, but some of his compatriots did. His tales were fascinating.

After two hours of walking we encountered another river, a real one this time, flowing like fury. Ra was going west, he said, and I told him I was going east, downstream.

"Thank you for the 'ceegarettes'," he said. "I wish to leave you with a small gift. Open it if you need warmth." He handed me a small stone box. It was too hot to hold, but I didn't want to offend him, so I burned my hand and set it quickly inside my pack with hardly a whimper.

"Thank you. I offer you the rest of my cigarettes." He nodded and took the pack from me, then turned and walked west, I leapt into the fast-flowing river and swam as fast as I could downstream. Which was, I admit, not all that fast or all that far, but when added to the current it was enough to escape the wildfire. I left the stream and continued, sopping wet and shivering, until I reached the bustling metropolis of Willow; 56 people and a payphone. Within two hours I was warming up in the back of my friend Dave's Honda, and on my way home.

In the end, the fire destroyed a few thousand acres, and was effectively extinguished after a week. My car was, as I expected, a charred wreck. I was safe though, and had an experience that I would never tell anyone about.

However cold I have gotten since then, I have never opened the box.

*James Parker PhD studied mathematics and computer science before ending up as a Professor of Art at the University of Calgary. His expertise ranges from computer simulation, image processing, artificial intelligence, game design, and generative art.*

## EXERCISES, CHAPTER EIGHT

1. Space. "Simulation" is paired with the artwork *Space* by Helena Hadala. To get an inkling of the expanse of space, our observable universe is equivalent to the distance that light has travelled since the beginning of time. Beyond our observable universe, there is likely much more — possibly even an infinite number of universes. To get a sense of the distance Aaron has travelled to get to Earth, relax and allow your consciousness to merge with the infinite nature of the cosmos. Expand further to align with the vastness of the entire universe, billions of light years in the distance, in every direction. Now try imagining infinite universes. Reflect on the complexities, take a step toward peace, release your ego. All things are possible.

2. Delayed Gratification. In "Local Smoke" Ra gives Mike a small stone box for warmth. No matter how cold Mike gets, he has never opens the box. Resisting temptation like this can lead to increased patience and greater awareness. As an experiment in delayed gratification, put off for a while opening a gift, or smoking a cigarette, or eating a piece of cake, or opening a text from someone who you really care for.

3. Mindfulness. In "Simulation," despite knowing the world will end soon, Ron carries on enjoying a good meal. Can you let go of how things should be and accept them as they are in that very moment? It's hard, but try to focus on just one thing at a time and be grateful for what you have now.

*For further study:*

Heinlein, Robert A. *Have Space Suit, Will Travel.* Scribner, 1958. Jim says "*Heinlein taught me, 'There is always someone smarter than you'.*"

Orwell, George. *1984.* Secker and Warburg, 1949. Jim says: *"Orwell taught me, 'Freedom is essential for creativity and progress'."*

# CONFLUENCE

*Images and Haiku by*

Helena Hadala RCA

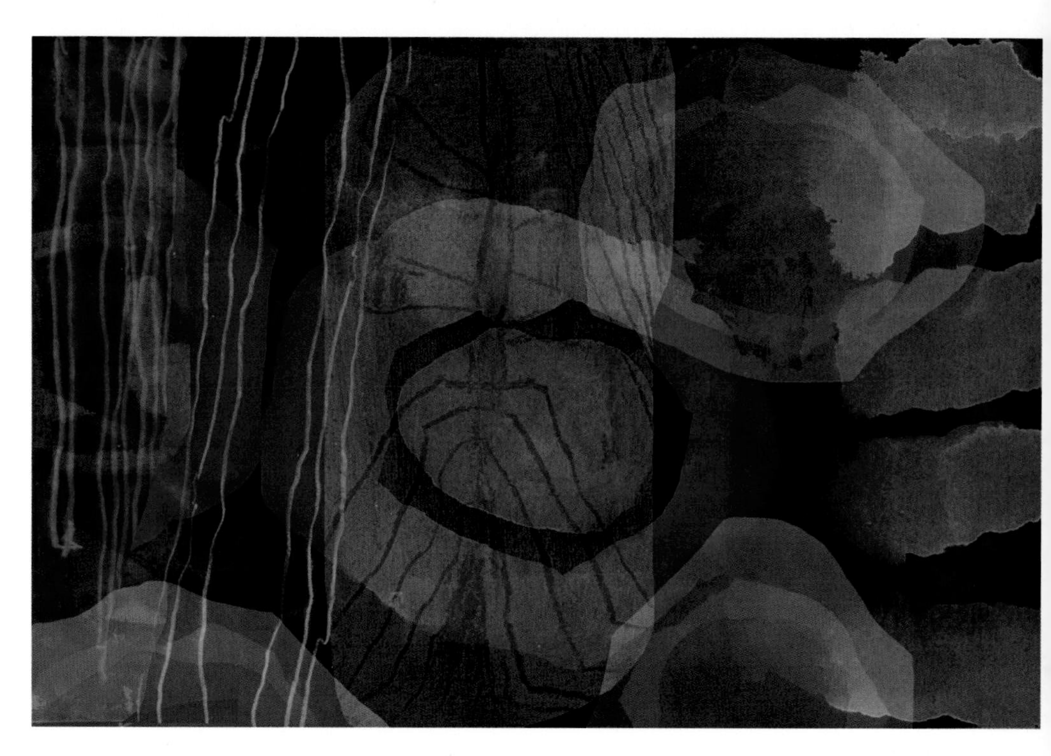

*TRANSFORMATION*

# CONFLUENCE

## *Images and Haiku by*

## Helena Hadala RCA

THE 18 SELECTED IMAGES illustrated in this book are part of a larger body of work entitled *Confluence*. This series, comprised of 36 visual images, was inspired by the poetry of Taoist author Deng Ming-Dao and was originally created for our collaborative, interdisciplinary project *Walking River.* For my contribution to *Walking River,* I created visual images to convey the connotation of each poem in an intuitive manner. My objective was to visually reflect rather than describe the meaning of the words, allowing for contemplation of the poetry to become visible and take on tangible form.

Deng Ming-Dao writes in his book *Everyday Tao*, "Tao is everywhere. It is literally the movement of all life. It is endless and flows in all directions. Since Tao is the total ongoing process of the universe, it makes sense to go along with it. If we swim in a river, we should make use of its current."

The images reflect the Taoist view that we are all following a spiritual path. They were initially created in my studio using mixed media elements such as gouache, watercolour, and crayon and then integrated with an image-editing program.

In *Embrace Your Divine Flow,* the Confluence images provide a supplementary pictorial component to the book. To continue with the notion of confluence, I have included my poetic response to complement each image in the form of haiku. The editors have thematically paired the images with the authors' stories to complement each of the chapters.

Hidden threads unravel
Circles around coalesce
The dance goes on

*The artwork "PATIENCE" accompanies chapter sixteen, Rich Théroux's story "Let The World Catch Up."*

Outside looking in
Waiting by the water's edge
Balanced counterpoise

*The artwork "PASSAGE" accompanies chapter two, Antoine Mountain's story "Spirits of the Departed."*

*PATIENCE*

*PASSAGE*

Outside boundaries
A restful sanctuary
All illusions fade

*The artwork "BOUNDARIES" accompanies chapter six, John Heerema's story "Kick. Step. Kick. Step."*

Whispers of silence
Unravel mysteries
Listen with intent

*The artwork "DELIGHT" accompanies chapter fourteen, Audrya Chancellor's story "Atlantean Illumination."*

*BOUNDARIES*

*DELIGHT*

Water comes and goes
Following the ebb and flow
With full abandon

*The artwork "GRATITUDE" accompanies chapter fifteen, Iikiinayookaa Marlene Yellowhorn's "The Sacred Places Stories Take Us."*

Peeling the onion
Seeing into one's nature
Rock, paper, scissors

*The artwork "MASK" accompanies chapter five, Kayla Lappin's story "The Veil."*

*GRATITUDE*

*MASK*

Just before dawn
Dark sky full of emptiness
The message is clear

~

*The artwork "FREEDOM" accompanies chapter eleven, Hilda Chasia Smith's story "Felina Aloha's Evolution."*

Sweet liberation
The flutter of a heartbeat
Pulsating with life

~

*The artwork "BREATHE" accompanies chapter four, Julian Hobson's story "Mother Son."*

*FREEDOM*

*BREATHE*

Spirit moves through me
Subtle energies unite
Eternal rhythms

~

*The artwork "SOUND" accompanies chapter three, Islene Runningdeer's story "Nenet's Broken Heart."*

Water flows
Undercurrent of desire
Traverses the divide

~

*The artwork "BRIDGE" accompanies chapter thirteen, Lynda Partridge's story "Tough Love."*

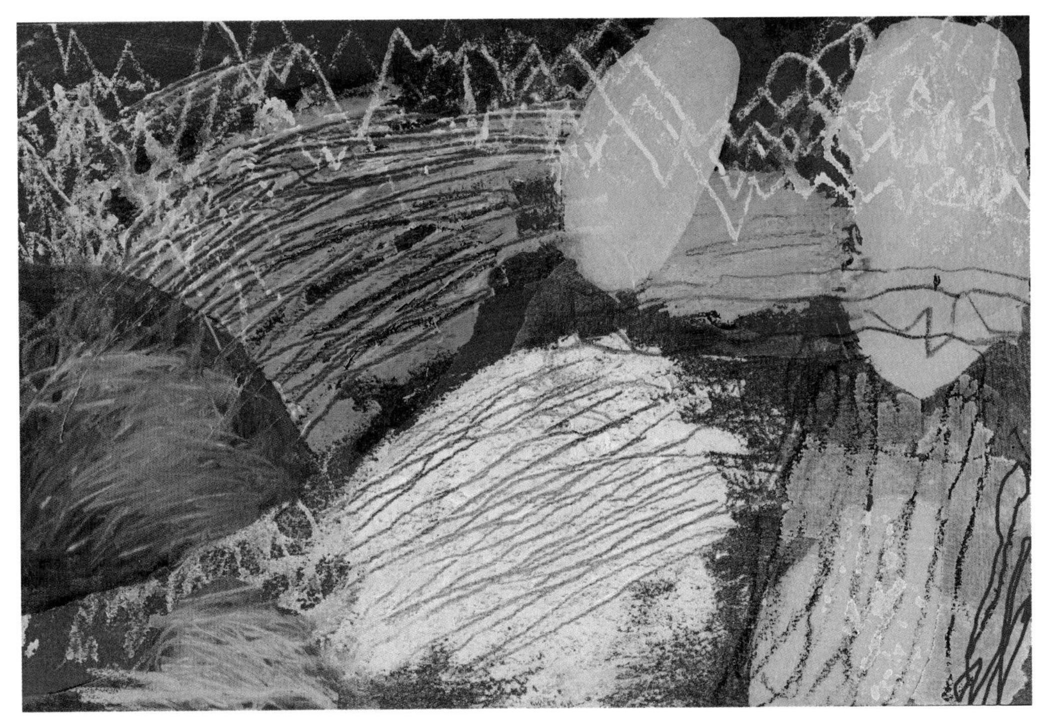

*SOUND*

*BRIDGE*

Beneath the surface
Hidden virtuosity
All is potential

~

*The artwork "SPACE" accompanies chapter eight, James R. Parker's story "Simulation." "*

A fragmented mind
Birds twitter in unison
The shadow follows

~

*The artwork "SURRENDER" accompanies chapter one, Mar'ce Merrell's story "Water Calls, Water Holds."*

*SPACE*

*SURRENDER*

Opaque and obscured
Mystery envelops me
The darkness brings light

*The artwork "NOTHING" accompanies chapter nine, Lorene Shyba's story "Aura Borealis."*

Graceful interlude
Flow of continuity
Restores confidence

*The artwork "INTERVAL" accompanies chapter nine, James R. Parker's story "Local Smoke."*

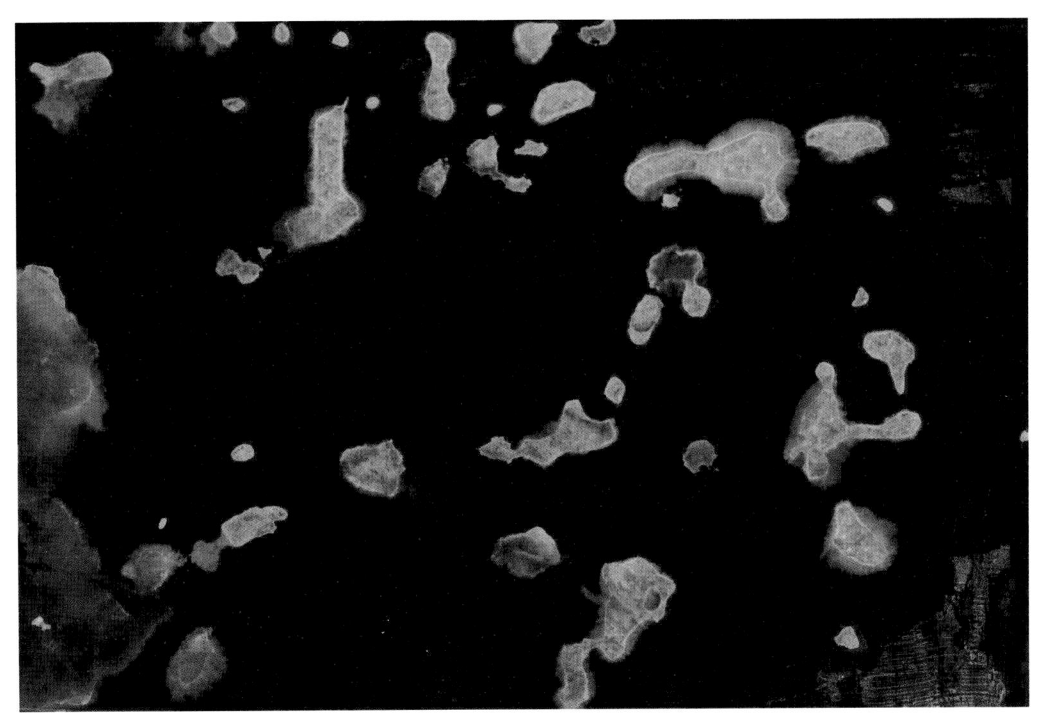

*NOTHING*

*INTERVAL*

Consciousness holds true
Harmony in trinity
Body, mind, and soul

*The artwork "HOME" accompanies*
*chapter twelve, Raymond Yakeleya's story*
*"The Mountain, the Wind, and the Wildflowers."*

Seamless divisions
Ditto above and below
Refined strata

*The artwork "DUALITY" accompanies*
*chapter ten, Alex Soop's story*
*"Niisitapi Reveal."*

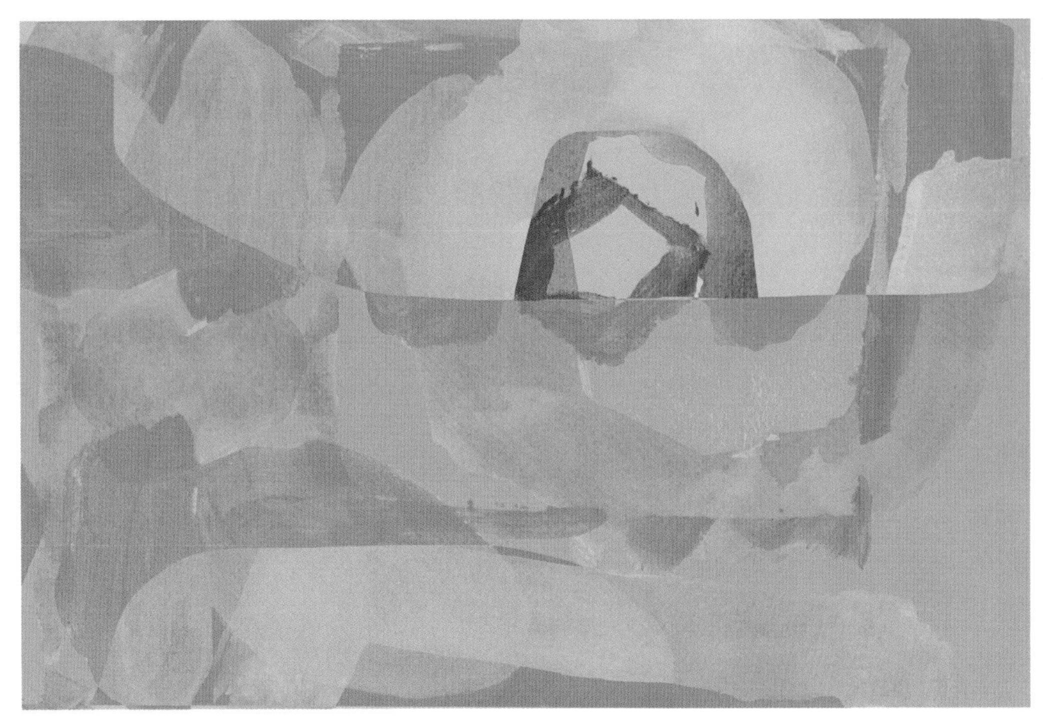

*HOME*

*DUALITY*

## *FLOW*

In the composition entitled *Flow*, my intent was to create a harmonic composition to echo unity inherent in opposites. The fluid calligraphic lines imply 'flow' and seemingly connect in the centre of the image to unify the strong division created by the contrasting dark and light sides. The calligraphic line maintains flow whether one is in a dark (sad, stressful) or light (joyful, happy) situation in life.

The Sufi saying, "The ocean refuses no river," is a profound metaphor for our lives. To me, this idiom offers hope and encouragement to use one's inherent ability to flow through life, to not be attached to joy or sorrow, but to just accept what is. I often wonder when I find myself sitting at the edge of the river of life, just watching and fearful of stepping in, why I am holding back from the inevitable assimilation into that peaceful ocean? And other times, when I do find the courage to enter the river and end up frantically swimming up stream, I ask myself, "Why not float?"

*— Helena Hadala RCA*
*Calgary, Alberta, 2023*

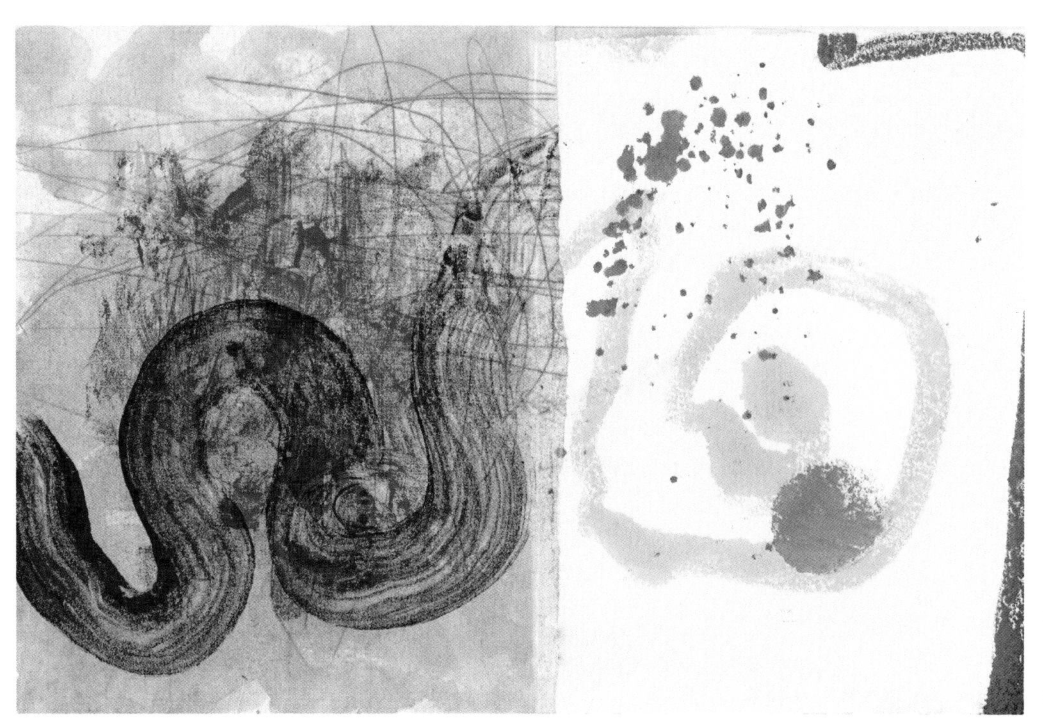

*FLOW*

*The artwork "Flow" accompanies chapter seven, Valerie Campbell's story "Moving Her Poetic Body."*

## NINE

# AURA BOREALIS

*Lorene Shyba*

JAKE

*I had no idea Marty's experiment with infinity would help me so much with the pain.*

In shock and detached from my battered body I hover above the sad scene that unfolds below. My truck, crumpled against the mountain, is a twisted wreck, radio still blares. Spooked by a near collision, caribou and their calves scramble off the highway into the forest, lit by weird colours in the sky. Marty races along the highway, shouting, "Hey! Stop! He's trapped!" The screeching of tires and a dog barking echo in the night.

Marty's urgent cries jolt me from my daze into a world of pain. Caught up in the wreckage, my leg is in fucking agony.

"Patches, go find!" a woman's voice commands, followed by running, stomping and more barking.

"C'mon, Jake, brother up," Marty's voice quivers. She presses on, "Shitty luck, eh? But there's a lady here who's gonna get you out, you'll see."

My sister Marty and me...what are the crappy odds our partners would dump us at the same time. Now our lovesick road trip is in the toilet too.

I feel rough hands as a woman hitches a rope around my shoulders. How the hell did she end up here?

"Push!" the woman screams at me, then to Marty, "Pull!"

The woman fastens her dog to the rope too, adding strength.

She bellows at Marty or perhaps her dog—I can't tell. "Put your back into it, goddammit!"

"Help!" I yell. "My leg is pinned under the fucking steering column. It's going to rip right off."

"Cut the damn seatbelt!" the woman shouts, thrusting a hunting knife into Marty's hands. Wildly sawing, Marty sets me free.

"This is it now, buddy," the woman says. "Squirm out. Push!"

As I scrape and tumble through the sunroof, the ever practical Marty snatches the keys from the ignition and turns off The Weeknd, mid-phrase, *Ooh, I'm drowning in the night—*

I collapse on the ground like a lifeless sack and they haul me into the back of the lady's Jeep, onto a mound of furs. Flashes of conversation: "Double back to the hunting camp ... No point trying to patch him up in the ditch ... Helping the Elders with their traplines..." The lady's name must be 'Jezz', and her dog is 'Patches'. Marty drones on and on about her no-good ex.

We bump along on back roads for what feels like forever until we come to a clearing with a clay-chinked log cabin. Marty and Jezz drag me out the back hatch and roll me out onto the ground. Patches runs around barking at the edge of the forest.

Weakly, I find my voice. "Is the sky dancing, or am I losing my mind?"

"Welcome to the land of the living, Mr. Jake!" Jezz exclaims. "Come on get up." Pain shoots through my leg but they manage to set me upright. "I'm Jezz," she says, "pleased to meet you. I'm an anthropologist by trade not a physicist, but as for those northern lights, you're not losing your marbles. I reckon you know how a neon tube glows red when gas atoms get all excited by electricity?" They lead me toward a treed area in the yard. Hard to concentrate on the science lesson when all I can think about is the pain and how I have to pee.

Jezz goes on, "When struck by solar particles, atoms and molecules in the atmosphere emit colourful wavelengths." She gestures at the sky and despite nearly falling over, I look up again at the waving curtains of green and purple light. I grab hold of what looks like an old dog sled, prop myself up, unzip, and relieve myself. "Keeps the Sasquatch at bay," I offer as an embarrassed explanation.

"Just the opposite, if you want the truth," Jezz says and then drowns out the sound of my waterfall with a jolly navy ditty. "Next time, head on over there," Jezz points in the direction of a shack across the clearing with a moon cut in the door. Marty, heeding her own call of nature, makes a drama of holding her nose and trotting off into the dark. Jezz hobbles with me over to some hammocks strung out in the yard. She boosts me up and tucks me in under a striped Hudson Bay blanket, injured leg exposed.

"No blood, that's the main thing," Jezz whispers. "By a stroke of luck, I was there for you today. This treatment will help stabilize things." She hovers one hand over my leg and the other over my abdomen. "It's like this," she says. "Just as the northern lights carry an electrical charge, particles within your body do too. They're influenced by colour vibrations and electromagnetic fields. Feel it?"

In that moment, a thought crosses my mind—can she heal my broken relationship too? I quickly shake free of that notion.

"Here's what you do next," Jezz continues. "Relax and play a game with the colours and energy in the sky. Cup your hands in front of your face and visualize an invisible sphere to draw in the power of the dancing colours, what I call the 'aura borealis'. Sprinkle your thoughts and ambitions inside. Teach this to your sister too, and it will give you guys something to do while I warm up the cabin." She whistles for Patches.

"Yep, Patches and I are heading in to scramble up some eggs and toast," she informs me. "It'll take time; stove's cold."

Patches, back from guard duty, barks when he hears his name. Jezz, still humming the navy ditty throws a biscuit at Patches and tosses me a couple of granola bars.

I vaguely wonder how Jezz knows navy ditties and what Marty will think of her strange instructions.

MARTY

*I had no idea Jake's pain would help me out so much with the shatter of my lost love.*

With the bright colours flickering in the sky, it's an easy stumble back to the hammocks from the outhouse. Patches scared away the biggest of the critters from the yard, hope so anyway, but there is scurrying all around, maybe martens or wolverines? Clever ones that know how to avoid Jezz's traps.

Who woulda thought that both Jake and I would get dumped by our partners at the same time? I feel stupid, worthless, and godawful lonely. Instead of hassling Jake about the crash and my insecurities though, I grab one of the striped blankets like the one he's wrapped in, climb into the other hammock, and stare at the sky. He tosses me a granola bar.

"How are you holding up, bro?" I ask him.

"If I lay here real still I might be alive in the morning," he mumbles with a mouthful of crunchy granola. "Listen, Marty, I'm sorry about the accident."

"Caribou on the road, I mean, licking the highway? Who knew." I rip open my granola bar, pause for a moment, and add a thought. "It was like she was waiting for us. Dr. Jezz, I mean. What's with that?

"She's a doctor?" Jake mumbles and crunches.

"Sort of, in bone hunting and religious studies or something. Told me in the Jeep on the way over here she was working with the Elders on ancient mammoth remains, go figure, and they put her to work on their trapline. More limber than they are, she said. Where'd you say she went just now?"

"She's lighting the stove ... cooking eggs, casting spells?" Jake hesitates. "She might be a witch, Marty, but that's cool, isn't it?"

"Earth to Jake. A witch? Maybe a healer?"

We go quiet, munching granola, gazing at the coloured curtains churning up the sky, ruminating on memories of our exes. How could it possibly be otherwise?

"Marty," he asks me, his voice weary, "you ever heard about northern lights being called 'aura borealis'?

"You mean 'aurora borealis'? Maybe you heard her wrong?"

"Jezz said 'aura borealis' because colours possess some kind of medicine power, or energy, or something. I'd explain more but God, I'm wiped out and my leg hurts like a son of a bitch."

I urge him on anyway.

"Okay," Jake says, "she said bring your hands together and invite aura borealis..." He trails off, mumbling some more about relaxing, it's a game of invisible spheres, storing memories, and so on. I give it a go, forming a sphere with my hands close to my face. I beckon the colour energy of the greens and purples from the swirling sky. I can tell Jake is drifting off to sleep but I try to get a story from him to place into the sphere, as Jezz suggested.

"Best memory?" he asks. "Probably when we used to jump in the river and ride the current, then dad would fish us out. Remember that from when we were kids?"

"Mostly you did, but yeah, I jumped in a few times." I say, wiggling my fingers to pop his memory into the sphere. "How about a wish, an ambition?" I ask.

"Easy," he says. "I wish my fucking leg gets better."

I don't blame him, poor guy. If it wasn't such a lost cause, he'd probably wish for his heartbreak to vanish too.

Then it's my turn. "My best memory is from when we were kids too, flying down to Vancouver, first time in a plane. Remember that? You were playing Nintendo and mom and dad were snoozing but I remember feeling energized—like anything in the world was possible. A wish? Well," I say to Jake, "I'll double down on your wish about your fucking leg getting better."

I don't bother wishing about my own ex either. Lost cause.

Then, I launch the energy ball into space with made-up math equations behind it that I reckon will make it go twice as fast every second all the way to the edge of the universe, catapulting into space in a straight line, all the way to infinity.

Except...it doesn't.

Instead, a void darker than dark, devoid of all form and energy transforms all around into an infinity of nothing, no beginning, no end—peaceful and perfectly still. It is an expanse of nothing that holds within it the potential for everything. In this contraction of blackness, this perfectly absorbent, velvety blackness, colours and light have not arrived, nor has time. There is no time.

In this absolute blackness, where colours and light have yet to arrive and time does not exist, I find myself explaining the essence of this void to another, perhaps-stronger version of myself, who listens intently. I whisper to my enraptured listener, *You may be a hallucination, but you are connected with me. I feel you.* The good listener remains neutral, shrouded in stillness, effortlessly absorbing the musings of my mind. Amidst this tranquility, the sounds of the forest, the cabin's smoke, and Jake's breath persist in my awareness. Yet, for my listener, there are no distractions to disturb her profound repose.

After a time, or no time, vibrations within and amidst this infinite space of stillness begin to flourish with spiritual power. Behind my closed eyes, I sense the aura of the borealis, the layered dance of the Goddess, granting glimpses of creativity and courage. I merge with my enraptured listener in a blissful union.

The frequency of colours that were held in check by the stillness of the black void now cascade and unfurl into a shimmering tapestry within the infinite expanse, seething to release the everything that the void was withholding. Time does not pass; there is only an eternity of simultaneous existence.

Like a hologram across my consciousness, a vision comes to me of being a child on an airplane with my family, soaring through the air and knowing I can do anything I want in life. Memories of my ex-lover becomes mere chatter that I render invisible. I am seeing more clearly now, present and connected, feeling alone but not lonely amidst the flickering array of colours. The colours suddenly converge and explode into radiant white light, transforming the intimate space of dark reflection into brilliant expansion. This blinding light yearns to fill the entire space around me, then the atmosphere, into the stratosphere, and to every corner of the universe. But the memories and desires encapsulated within the sphere pulsate with a longing to be actualized. Like a finely spun, resplendent cocoon, this sphere of luminous energy envelops both Jake and me in our hammocks, providing protection. I reach out and take his hand.

JEZZ

The cabin cook stove is fired up and hot. Jezz stirs the eggs and grinds on a sprinkle of pepper. She twirls around to retrieve a loaf of sourdough, kneeling down to scratch Patches' ears.

"Nearly time for you to round up our guests for growlies," she remarks to the dog, who springs towards the door upon hearing the words "outside" and "growlies." Patches figures there might be something good to eat, or at least chase, out there in the yard.

Jezz slides the cast iron pan off the heat and crosses over to the window. Her gaze fixates on the swirling, kaleidoscopic cocoon of protection nestled among the hammocks.

"Hey, wait a sec, Patches, come look see, there's a glow out there in hammockland. The girl is playing the infinity game, or maybe they both are!"

Patches trots across the room, his claws tapping on the wooden floor, and leaps onto the back of the wingback chair by the window. He nudges the curtains aside with his nose, pressing it against the glass as he whines.

"They've set up good intentions to get Jake's bum leg back in shape, that's for sure. Maybe even patching up their loneliness and broken hearts. We'll see if the cosmos is aligning to unveils its best healing tricks," she chuckles, taking a sip of tea.

"Nope, definitely not time to bring them in yet," she tells the dog. A swirling bubble encases the siblings. A fluid, rope-like shine connects them to each other and to nature all around—an iridescent silver sheen that emits a sparkling rose hue.

JAKE

Detached again, I'm in a dream, but I know I'm in a dream. A vision of Jezz is here and I accept her presence as being true. I have faith in the message she brings: "Cheer up, don't be the victim, there is rapture and clarity in your individual flow." I trust that she will be a brilliant guide. With a beckoning gesture, she leads me towards the billowing clouds, soaring high above a tumultuous river. I survey the churning rapids below.

A caribou bows her antlers and drifts by in a vision of light on the riverbank, thanking me for sparing her life and that of her calf. I watch myself jump into the river, and suddenly I'm right there in the icy water, surrendering to its flow.

Dad appears and I feel strong arms pulling me from the rapids, wrapping me in a towel, like a rebirth. "Begin again, with intensity, love, and trust," Dad imparts. He points back upstream and adds, "There are plenty of fish…" I know what he means and savour his words and the soft orb of his comfort.

Suddenly, Marty sends a buzz of warmth through my hand, and my body vibrates with love and wellbeing. Rainbow hues settle all around, and I feel each energy field extending tendrils of radiance and healing upon my injured leg. From behind my eyelids I perceive these colours exchanging power with the aura borealis. I drop into a deep peace of velvety nothingness.

MARTY

From around the edges of our reverie I hear Jezz yell, "Hey you two, tea and eggs!" Patches barks like crazy and as I crack my eyes open, I see him running full tilt across the yard. Jake swings up from his hammock and plants his feet to brace himself for the joyful dog. His leg is apparently no longer in anguish.

"Patches, whoa, there's a good boy!" Patches body checks Jake, nearly knocking him over.

"I forgot to warn you, Patches like to hug," Jezz chuckles, approaching us with open arms. She embraces Jake in a heart-to-heart that ends with three big thumps on the back and a shove in the direction of the cabin. Patches spins in circles. Jake flashes a peace sign.

"Not a trace of a limp. Good work, team. We were all at the right place at the right time, my friends," insists Jezz. "Jake, grab an armload of wood on your way in, and oh, make some toast."

Jake responds, "If you help us peel the truck off the side of the mountain, I'll do extra chores tomorrow." He walks backward, hoping for a confirming "yep" from Jezz.

"Yep," Jezz retorts. "There are chores on the trapline, plenty!"

She turns her gaze back to me, speaking softly. "How are you, Martina? I expect you have some reflecting to do on what happened out here in hammockland?"

She knows my name is Martina? I swing to the ground, exhale, drop my chin, and shuffle my feet around, feeling slightly embarrassed about how much Jezz knows or may even be responsible for the spiritual connections I felt.

"Truth is, it was intense," I manage to utter. "I mean, the velvet universe with its no-nonsense of love and clarity...Jezz, do you think I helped Jake heal, or was I imagining—"

"Overspill of love," she explains. "When you fully open yourself to love, as you have, you expand your capacity to love and heal others."

As I lean back against the dogsled, she hooks her right hand under my chin and pivots my face up toward the sky. The northern lights have almost folded up their light show, revealing stars and constellations stretching out forever into the complexity of infinity.

"The same overspill principle goes for beauty. When you cultivate the experience of beauty, you expand your capacity to experience and share the beautiful."

"Beauty...expansiveness... I'm all ears," I reply, captivated by her wisdom.

Gratefully, she carries on. "The intelligence that created this wondrous universe resides within you—as you, in fact. Pay attention to the universe around us tonight, Martina. By being a good listener, being aware, embracing beauty, and expanding love, you can tap into the potency of your transformed self — solitary but never plagued by loneliness."

The colours of the aura borealis flicker softly now and sounds of the night echo and chirp. I feel invigorated, and fiercely awakened. I can even smell toast burning from all the way across the yard and hear Jake cursing in frustration.

"Um, you're not in a big hurry to get rid of us, are you, Jezz? For one thing, I could use a good teacher, and it seems Jake could benefit from further lessons in the art of toasting."

*I had no idea Dr. Jezz's games with infinity would help me out so much with my messed-up life.*

*Lorene Shyba MFA PhD is a mapper of information and a builder of knowledge. She is publisher at Durvile & UpRoute Books near Diamond Valley, Alberta where she is series editor of the Every River Lit, Reflections, and True Cases series. She co-edits the Indigenous Spirit of Nature series with Raymond Yakeleya. Her greatest joy comes from being a good friend, a good mother, and an active listener.*

## EXERCISES, CHAPTER NINE

1. NOTHING. "Aura Borealis" is paired with *Nothing* by Helena Hadala. Being matched with the art *Nothing* is an interesting challenge because when is 'nothing' a good thing? When it is a refreshing springboard for creativity, of course. Do you need more stillness and peace in your life? Try sitting quietly, breathing slowly in on a count of 4 and out on a count of 8. Take a moment at the end of each exhale and each inhale to clear your mind of thoughts and experience the aliveness of just being.

2. FORGIVENESS. Marty and Jake both install frontline wishes and backstory wishes into the energy sphere before they try launching it into infinity. Their frontline wish is to heal Jake's leg, but their backstory wishes involve their broken love affairs. Take a minute and think about how forgiveness might factor into healing a broken relationship. Can you forgive the other person? Can you forgive yourself? Take your time.

3. RECIPROCITY. Do you have brothers or sisters? Or do you have people in your life who are close to you like a brother or a sister? Visualize the love for this person who shares this reciprocal, unconditional love. Write them a note that you can share with them in person, or as a phone call, or a letter, or even a text. Let them know how important they are to you and how much you care for them, through thick and thin.

Suggestions for further study:

Wallis, Christopher D. *Tantra Illuminated: The Philosophy, History, and Practice of a Timeless Tradition.* Mattamayura Press, 2012.

Brennan, Barbara Ann. *Core Light Healing: My Personal Journey and Advanced Concepts for Creating the Life You Long to Live.* Hay House, 2017.

TEN

# NIITSITAPI REVEAL

## *Alex Soop*

THIS IS A PERSONAL STORY that I must tell. Or, at least, to put into words for someone else to read one day. Plain and simple. It is a startling account of my experiences while field researching my blood lineage. It began with a trip I put together in hopes of quenching a longing I had to understand the sacred lives of my First Nations ancestors. It's like I needed to bring the dualities of my life together: the white English me and Indigenous me that were not fully connected. I knew in my heart that I could count on discoveries in the New World to reveal my full identity.

Even though I was born and raised in the great and noble country of England, I have Blackfoot blood coursing through my veins. My great-grandfather was a brave man of the Blood Tribe, hailing from an area called Bullhorn. Like many of his mates, my great-grandfather decided he would find excitement and adventure in the Great War, off in faraway lands. Exciting undertakings that reserve life couldn't provide were awaiting them if they enlisted in the Canadian Expeditionary Force, fighting boldly in the trenches of the Western Front. So, he and others from the Blood Tribe willingly enlisted.

Before ultimately being sent to the front lines, my great-grandfather spent a wee bit of time posted in England; where the CEF was based, along with The British Armed Forces. In a small Manchester pub, great-grandfather met the woman who would become my great-grandmother. The rest, as they say, is history.

Canada was my only intended destination: Alberta and British Columbia, but last-minute plans had me incorporate Alaska into this trip. My reading and studies on the Na-Dene Peoples of the Pacific Northwest intrigued me about the State of Alaska. I supposed I would start there, then make my way southeastward through the Rocky Mountains until I arrived at the plains region of my lineage — the Blackfoot, or, as I had discovered in researching the Blackfoot tongue, Niitsitapi.

I worked like a dog to be allotted the time off I required for my journey to Canada. I asked for two months off without pay, and my boss said yes, given all the work I had done for a year without taking any time off.

My initial stop and the first leg of my journey began in Juneau, Alaska. I found it disheartening that I didn't happen upon any local Indigenous people. I became a regular at some of the local hot-spot pubs for the three days I spent there. I then came across a brown-skinned fellow who I was sure was an Alaskan First Nation person. No luck there with the lad. He was of Mexican descent and had moved north from Houston, Texas not some two years prior. Damn, so close, I thought. But not close enough.

From Juneau, I made my way south, island hopping across the Alexander Archipelago. I was quite blissful, to say the least, when I finally came across some of the local Tlingit People scattered amongst the islands. They found my accent and dialect quite splendid, even though it's from the working-class midlands of England. Their manner of speech was interesting too, and unlike any other Caucasian Americans I had come across thus far. I decided to stay a week when I found a Tlingit family willing to take me under their wing, inviting me to live in their dwellings.

I was given a brief lesson about their traditional ways of life. Just like us Brits, they too loved their seafood. I had a bloody good and unforgettable time. Along with my timely departure came the gift of a magnificently fabricated Chilcott blanket, a gift that would come in handy in the days to follow. I was sad to leave my Tlingit hosts.

Next up was Canada, which was easy enough to access because the Canada/US border line carved right through the cluster of islands connecting Juneau to the continental mainland. I ferried from Alaska to British Columbia and hitchhiked my way to the small city of Prince Rupert where I stayed the night in a modest hotel to gather myself and plan out the rest of my southeast journey down through the mountainous woodlands of British Columbia.

I used to spend whatever vacation time I could muster hiking, climbing, and camping out in the Scottish Highlands, but the BC landscape was much wilder. As an avid outdoorsman though, I was excited rather than intimidated. The crisp mountain air was like inhaling the breath of the Almighty. Nothing at all like the air in midland cities. Getting in good physical condition in the Highlands would play a major role in my trek between Prince Rupert and, ultimately, Calgary, Alberta.

While trekking down the side of the highway, I heard the sound of hissing brakes and blow-off pressure valves of an enormous semi-truck from behind me. The massive truck nearly jackknifed to a stop right in my path, making me dive into the deep, grassy ditch. I heard an offer and climbed aboard.

Good Samaritan Joseph noticed my big pack and decided to take a chance. I rode with him for over an hour before he slowed his speed near an offramp.

"Well, my exit is comin' up. I recommend you stay put and have yourself a gander at Barkerville. It's a remarkable little town," said Joseph.

"Why thank you, mate. I appreciate the gesture, but perhaps it's best that I keep on heading east before it gets too late."

"I hear you on that one." Joseph exited the turnpike and slowly pulled over to the shoulder of the highway. "Good luck, eh," he said and extended his arm in a good-mannered gesture.

"Thank you, Joseph. Cheers and best wishes," I said as I

shook his hand in appreciation. And just like that, another good-hearted Canadian was out of my life.

Following the last of a number of rides I thumbed through BC and into Alberta, I waited alongside Highway 1 as a few cars sped past me before darting across the road. Keeping a good pace, I trekked down the grassy ditch of the highway, ultimately settling beneath an overpass to study my map and escape the dust of the road and the searing summer heat. I was doing my calculations on the length of time it would take to walk the rest of the way to Calgary when a truck pulled over.

"Hey there, stranger. You need a lift?" yelled a man through his passenger window.

I looked up in surprise, astounded at how kind and trusting these Canadians were to me. "Yeah," I yelled back, "I could most definitely use a lift." I climbed to my feet, jogged over to the truck, unshouldered my pack, and tossed it in the cargo box. As I hopped in I noticed a "Pow-Wow Fever" sticker on the glove compartment but it didn't carry any meaning for me at first glance.

"How do you do," I said, offering my hand in gratitude. "I'm Paxton."

"Holeh, an Englishman." He gripped my hand tightly. "I'm Tyson. Buckle up and let's get a-rollin'."

"Righty-ho," I said and then mimicked him good-naturedly, "Let's get a-rollin'."

"So, where y'off to, there, brother?" Tyson asked as he put the truck in gear and peeled off the gravel shoulder. He spoke with a slight accent, similar to the Tlingit people I had stayed with.

"Well, I'd like to get to Calgary, if you're heading that way?"

"Yes sir, I sure am — and then some."

"Beg your pardon, mate?"

"I'm just by-passing Calgary. I'm actually heading down south."

"South? You wouldn't happen to be going near the Blood Tribe or around there, would you?" I asked eagerly.

"No shit? That's exactly where I'm headed. That's where I'm from," he said with a chuckle.

I was overcome with delight. His accent and the pow-wow sticker now made total sense to me. He must be an Indigenous man. "Well, I'll be … it truly is a small world after all."

"Sorry?" asked Tyson.

"Hmm, where to start." I pondered for a moment, trying not to betray my excitement. "I'll just come out and say it. I'm headed to the Blood Tribe too. You see, my great-grandfather hailed from there."

Tyson shot me a sideward glance. "Well holy shit on a stick. Bet you're glad I came along then, eh?"

"Very. Where are you coming from, if you don't mind my asking?"

"Wedding up in Banff—my sister's wedding. I was in the lineup, and now just making my way home. Boy I'll tell you what though, I'm sure as hell feeling the effects from last night."

"Was it a traditional wedding?" I inquired.

"I dunno what your concept of a traditional wedding is. But yeah, you can say that there was some tradition. We had a drum group sing, and an Elder bless the ceremony. The booze part wasn't quite as much tradition, though."

"Did the groom wear a headdress or something?"

Tyson burst out laughing so hard he nearly lost his grip on the steering wheel. Once he'd regained his composure, he asked, "Where did you say you were from, again?"

"I didn't. I hail from the city of Manchester, born and raised… Northern part of England."

"Well, that figures. I'll tell you something right quick, though," Tyson said. He eyed me and waited for me to acknowledge him. "Well, first of all, not any regular Joe Schmoe Indian is allowed to sport a headdress. It must be gifted to them, or they would have to earn it. And not to mention, my sister married a napikwaan, so yeah, there you go."

"Sorry. A napee—"

"Napikwaan," snickered Tyson, "it means 'white man' in Blackfoot."

"Ahh. My first Blackfoot language lesson."

"So, your great-grandfather? Let me guess. One of the few wars that Canada has been involved in?"

"That's right," I said, "World War One." I stopped and waited for instructions for me to enlighten him further. While waiting, I briefly examined Tyson. He didn't look at all like the warriors from the pictures I had studied in school. He was brawny, like he was a regular gym-goer. His chiselled jawline complimented his dark-brown hair, which was cut short, and pomaded into a faded Caesar cut. Although he was light-skinned, there was still some natural tan to him.

He nodded at me as if to say: carry on. And I did.

"My great-grandfather came from a place called Bullhorn—" I began.

"Gee, it just keeps getting better and better, don't it! That's the section of the rez where I'm from." He tittered like a schoolboy. "Sorry, go on."

I related the story of how my Blackfoot forefather had yearned for adventure and had enlisted in the Canadian Armed Forces with his brothers and fellowship. And then how it came to be that he met my great-grandmother. It didn't end there. Tyson was very interested to know how I grew up. The differences between my coming of age and his rez upbringing, his own words, were substantial.

The remaining leg of our flat prairie-land journey was filled with stories of myself and of Tyson. We started from our toddler years chatting about differences between rez life, and Manchester life and ended by comparing Blackfoot women with English women. From Tyson's description, I longed to meet a beautiful, caramel-skinned Blackfoot woman with flowing, jet-black hair, and narrowed eyes that pierced the soul.

"Wow. The Rocky Mountains look even more so beautiful when we're this far from them," I said, staring at the bedazzling sight of where the crimped, grey mountain slopes mingled into the indigo skyline.

"Yeah, eh? It means we're just about home sweet home whenever I gaze upon those lusty mountains."

"We're about there, then? At the reservation?" I wondered how mountains could be lusty but did not bring it up in conversation.

"Mmhmm, but around here, we just call it the rez, short for reserve. But just one stop before we header in, if you don't mind? It's a tradition for me."

"What do you have in mind, mate?" I asked. "A beer," Tyson brusquely said.

"Alright. I could use a pint."

The bar was called Queens. It was a local hotspot, being one of the only bars in the crossroads town of Fort Macleod. It was unlike the pubs I was used to back home. I was accustomed to a usual set-up of a sprawling bar table extending down a space that took up a quarter of the pub. My local watering hole back home had a charming, old-timey medieval feeling to it. In contrast, this Queens bar had a small, dingy tabletop bar, with only a few vacant chairs. Most of the patrons were scattered about, sitting around small tables with high-top stools sucked under them. The tiny dance floor was devoid of dancers, but country music blared anyway. Tyson and I found ourselves an empty stall in the back, a few feet from the lone billiards table and coin-operated jukebox.

"Hey, Tyson. Good to see ya bro," a tall man called out. He wore tattered blue jeans with a striped, button-up shirt, a black cowboy hat and a shiny buckled belt wrapped around his waist. I was to learn it was a championship rodeo buckle.

"Oh shit, if ain't my favourite cowboy: Johnny Walker," said Tyson, adding a rude snicker. "Tsaa, as if, this guy. Don't even start with that, hey," said Johnny. "Mind if I take a seat?" Without a reply, he pulled out a chair and plopped himself down.

Tyson nodded with a smile and turned to me. "You know how he got the name, Johnny Walker?"

I smiled and shook my head.

"Because he spends more time walking in the corral than he does actually riding the damn bull," laughed Tyson, giving the wobbly table a powerful smack.

I smiled and nodded courteously. I really didn't want to laugh crudely, for fear of angering this six-foot-something bull rider who'd just taken a seat at our table. "Good evening, mate, I'm Paxton. How do you do," I said with an outstretched arm.

"Oh yeah, this is Paxton. My apologies," said Tyson, pausing to clear his throat.

"So, you're an English feller, or something?" said Johnny. He snatched my hand in his and gave it a firm, twisting handshake.

"I am," I said.

"You know, my great-great-grandfather was from Ireland," said Johnny. "Hell, lemme buy you a beer. Hope you English boys like real beer." He got up from his seat and vanished toward the bar without taking in an answer from me.

"Charming lad," I said to Tyson.

"Ahh, don't let his thickness get to ya. He just fell off a few too many bulls and horses is all. Hell, he's prolly even been kicked by a few too many, too," said Tyson.

"What do ya figure? A few beers then be back on our way?" I asked.

"You betcha. I just need a few jiggles of a leg to shake this damn hangover."

There really is no such instance as a few beers. Even back home in England, the old saying is more jibber jabber than fact. I wasn't one to complain that night though. In a matter of no time, our table was full of local Indian cowboys, and they were all more than delighted to buy the foreign Englishman a few rounds. So, I figured I would stay a while and drink with them and listen to their stories of lives as Indian cowboys.

But good times were never meant to last—especially when

the alcohol was flowing freely. It wasn't too far into our evening when a fight broke out between Tyson and Johnny, and it was all over who owned a more powerful truck. Silly, really. Of course, we were tossed out into the parking lot on our arses.

"Come on, I know where there's a party. It's not far from here," slurred Tyson, his breath reeking of Budweiser and whiskey.

"Bloody hell, you're not good to drive, mate," I said, wobbling on my feet more than a little.

"No-o-o, not even, bro. I'm wicked good to go. I just had a few beers is all. Peanuts. Now come on, the girls are waiting on us."

"You know, my cousin once got into a nasty car accident. He too thought he'd only had a few and was good to drive. But no, that was not the case. Now he's in a wheelchair for life." "Well, I'll tell you what. You drive," he said, pointing at me while digging through his pockets with his other hand for his keys.

"Nope, not a good idea, mate. I had a few too many, and besides, I don't have a licence to drive in this country."

"Come on, bro, don't be such a puss. We'll backroad it. Won't even see no cops."

"Still not a good idea," I strongly asserted. But I clearly saw that there would be no persuading him.

"Okay then, how about this. I'll go and pick up the girls, and we'll come back for you."

"Your call," I said reluctantly. I had the distinct feeling Tyson would not be coming back for me. A good hunch, as it happened.

"Alright bro. I'll be right back, right quick."

Shaking my head in disapproval, I watched as Tyson drunkenly climbed aboard his raised pickup truck, starting it up and revving it hard, making the motor growl like a wild animal. I then watched a black police cruiser emerge from out of nowhere into the parking lot with a squeal of tires, cherries and blueberries activated for dramatic effect. Tyson was blocked in.

As much as I felt bad for poor Tyson about to be arrested, I was just glad he didn't get a chance to leave the parking lot behind the wheel—and in the state he was in.

I slipped into the shadows and carried on with my journey.

The night was cool, but the blacktop pavement radiated the day's absorbed summer heat. I headed eastward, strolling casually down what I figured was a deserted Main Street. The roadside side businesses were all interconnected, looking just like iconic buildings from wild west movies. In less than thirty minutes, I was at the margin of the town, the illumination from street lights dimming into blackness as the onslaught of the wild prairies emerged.

Not an hour into my walk, I badly wished that I had made a pit stop at the Mac's store for a bottle of water on the way out of town. The intoxicating effects of my few hours at the bar had disintegrated and I was left with a searing headache along with intense cottonmouth. The dry air of the prairie didn't help matters either.

My paced boot stomps and the buzz of nocturnal critters echoed through the cool night. Before long, an embracing melody of music drifted through the open atmosphere and enveloped my isolated senses. I stopped to have a listen. Still, I couldn't grasp where it was coming from. In the flat, remote distance were spread-out specks of light, what I presumed were separate reserve dwellings and farm acreages. Excitement once again brewed in the pit of my stomach. Water was on my mind. I continued forward with my steady stride. The music gradually grew louder with each set of footstep crunches on the gravel road. I picked up speed until I was almost at a full-tilt run.

At last, I could see a set of lights emerging from a lone building in the distance and I caught drifts of people talking and laughing. I smiled, slowed my pace and breathing, and strolled towards the light, thinking I might get a smidge of water.

As I approached the lone building, I could see it looked like an old-fashioned church. Two tall street lamps were positioned on each end of the gravel parking lot, their dull glow dousing the area in a gloomy orange tint. There were at least a dozen people or so standing about in small groups, drinking from bottles and smoking. Haphazardly parked cars littered the parking lot. Most of the vehicles looked too ancient to still be on the roads.

As I approached, a group that was outside chatting suddenly fell to dead silence. My footsteps on the gravel sounded eerie, even to me. The group's flickering cigarette cherries along with some dark shadows were the only indications of life. Once again, I could only hear crickets chirping and the ambiance of thumping music from within the building. I could feel cold gazes stabbing at me through the already-cool night.

I stepped cautiously forward and called out, "Umm, hello there. I'm sort of lost—I think," I said cautiously.

"Well, well, well. Would ya listen to that? Sounds like we got a Scotsman in our midst," said one of the men. I couldn't tell who the speaker was from the shadows enshrouding their faces.

"Uhh, yeah," I giggled uncomfortably. I figured now wasn't the time to correct the man and perhaps upset him—and his group of chums.

"I take it you're lost, eh?" said another man taking a leaping step from the group. "Well tellin' by your accent, you're wickedly lost." He broke out in a fit of laughter. The remaining group of men joined in.

"I am," I said.

They continued laughing at me as I stood motionless.

"Geez, you guys, can't you see he's lost and means us no harm? Now let's show him some hospitality," said a woman's voice. I hadn't noticed her and still couldn't see her face.

"Ehh, we're just teasin' him is all," blurted out a third, unknown man. He stepped out from the group and jogged toward me. At point-blank, he stopped right in front of me to light up a cigarette. The illumination from the lighter flame revealed his facial features. He looked exactly like the Indian men from my schoolbooks: long black hair that sailed past his powerful shoulders and black, almond eyes that looked like they had seen their fair share of skirmishes. Battle scars, I assumed, carved across his left cheek down to his well-formed chin.

My hands were sweaty and my heart hammered but I managed to say, "Hello."

"Oki, tsa niitapi?" he said.

"I beg your pardon?"

He broke out in a friendly chuckle. "I was just saying, hello, how are you?"

"Oh, okay. Another Blackfoot language lesson, then."

"Another?" he asked. In the dim lamplight I could see his black eyebrows rise.

"A fellow I got a ride from spoke Blackfoot," I said.

"Why'd he do that?" he asked. I could finally feel the coldness departing from his voice. "This is the Blood Tribe, right?" I asked.

"It is," said the man standing in front of me.

I replied to this with a bottomless sense of pride, "My great-grandfather was from this reserve."

The tension between us dissipated. "I'm Arthur. That guy is Ramsey, he's from Amskapi Piikuni, our Blackfeet cousins to the south." Arthur gestured to another person still in shadow.

"Chuffed to meet you, Arthur," I said, extending my hand to him.

"You drink?" asked Arthur. He clutched my hand and gave me an unfamiliar hand clasp.

"I would fancy some water, if you would have some?"

"There's prolly some inside. But for now, here, take this," said Ramsey. He shoved his way past the others and handed me a partially cold bottle of Budweiser. "Come on, let's drink," he said with a wide smile. "I've never drank me with no Scotsman."

I felt that I had warmed up enough to these gentlemen to politely correct him. "Actually, Ramsey, I'm from England."

"Oh okay, my apologies. So, you said your grandpa was from here? What was his name?" asked Ramsey. Like Arthur, his long black hair was tied in a tidy ponytail.

In no time, I was acquainted with the group of people standing outside. I was surrounded like a pack of wolves closing in for the kill. Only this pack didn't have a hungered eradication on their minds. They lined up and took turns stepping up to me and introducing themselves. Most of them had never once seen a foreign man step foot on the reserve lands—let alone share a beer with one. I was the centre of attention.

Following a few unfamiliar-tasting drinks, Arthur offered to take me inside to meet more people and even some of their Elders. I was informed that the occasion for the gathering was a wedding, a lively old merriment.

The wide-open, gymnasium-like interior was dimly lit. Candles placed upright in the centre of an arrangement of round tables danced and flickered. Colourful banners and traditional Blackfoot designs adorned the corners of the four walls. A lively band strummed their guitars and banged on a drum kit while the singer covered classic rock songs that I knew had been popular back in the day. Ramsey chaperoned me around the different tables of guests. I met a handful of couples and relatives—old and young alike. Each one was thrilled to hear that my great-grandfather was of their very own lineage. Some of the guests steered clear of me, gazing at me with rigidness, like I was a foreign animal in their domain. In a way, I was. From my studies I knew about the hardships suffered by First Nations Peoples as a result of French, then British colonization. I asked about kids and was told that there were none there due to the presence of alcohol. Fair enough.

Lastly, I was brought to the table reserved for the Elders. Some had their hair in braids and others wore swanky fedoras and cowboy hats. I was honoured to meet and greet such people who could trace their experience and family customs and ceremonies back to the early, traditional ways of life. They were just as thrilled to meet me. One of the older men told me he may have even fought in the same regiment as my great-grandfather. I felt privileged.

"Well, that should be about everybody, I'd say," said Arthur, showing me through to the brightly lit kitchen.

"I can't begin to thank you enough for welcoming me in. This is definitely one of the highlights of my trip thus far," I said.

"Man, don't even worry about it. It's our privilege, bro. Hell it's not every day that we get to come across a real-life Englishman." I raised my glass and Arthur lightly tapped it from top to bottom. I carried on through the night, drinking and exchanging stories with the people. In no time, my mind slipped from my full grasp on perception and into the blackened world of intoxication.

When I opened my eyes, I was in near-total darkness, minus the strips of dusty sunlight piercing into the room through the cracked margins of boarded-up windows. My blistered taste buds were swamped in a viscous taste of copper mingled with stale alcohol. Once again, I severely needed water.

I pushed off the stiff sofa I was sprawled across. A foul spray of dust and dirt exploded and hovered in the air, forcing me into a fit of coughing. I sat up to let my blurred eyes unite with my battered conscience. Wide awake, I stood up and immediately fell back down with shock. The room I was in was old. In fact, it was beyond old. It conveyed the look of countless abandoned years. The walls were tattered and broken, revealing crumbling drywall and inner studs of rotting wood. The floor was swathed in layers of grime, mould, and black muck.

I glanced at my watch. 11:07 a.m. July 17, 2008. Had I dreamt my night of fun? I couldn't have. I could still taste the sour traces of the potent liquor I had pounded back with my new friends, Arthur and Ramsay.

I stumbled through an open door to a darkened bathroom and lunged for it. I tried the faucets. They were tightly rusted in place, emitting a loud squeal as I twisted them with all my strength. Nothing came out. I tried the light switch. Nothing. Even the mirror was caked in years of grime and dust buildup.

Then I remembered my pack. I burst out of the bathroom and raked my head around the dusty room. My pack was nowhere. Panic arose in me like a gasoline-doused fire. I pushed my way through the double doors I remembered Arthur and Ramsey ushering me through last night. The doors swiveled on creaky, rusted hinges. It was as though they hadn't been used in years.

Out of the back kitchen, I recognized where I was. There were no intricate Blackfoot designs and decorative banners embellishing the hall. Only marred, brick-constructed walls stood upright with smears of black char and other unknown filth. Neatly organized tables were no longer in existence, replaced by heaps of burnt rubble and furniture remains. The large, open ballroom was dark except for puffs of dust glittering in light beams trickling in through scores of holes in the dilapidated roof like mini spotlights. The air was thick with the choking aroma of burnt wood and aged char.

I wasted no time and sprinted across the grand room toward the front entrance. From behind me I could still sense the coldness of unseen eyes gazing right through me. Like a crazed escapee, I burst out the front entrance doors and was immediately blinded by the downpour of the high-summer sun. Taking a few steps further away, I shielded my eyes and scanned the flat, grassy horizon. In the distance of wind-dancing grasses, I could see the movement of cars on a highway, progressing like small insects.

One last glance behind me, and I was off like a bat out of hell. The very sight of the charred remains of the building gave me gooseflesh. I ignored the searing desiccation in my throat and kept my legs moving until I felt I was well and safe enough away from the forsaken building.

And then I saw it. My eyes lit up like an explorer stumbling upon gold. There was my pack, sitting upright at the edge of the gravel road, half concealed by tall stalks of prairie grass. I snatched it up without stopping and bolted toward the T-intersection where the gravel met the blacktop. Once my boots touched the pavement, I stopped and unshouldered my bag. I always came prepared. Fishing through my pack, I seized my compass and kept on with my journey following the twist of the road heading southeast.

Walking against a breeze that had picked up from the direction of the rigid hedge of mountains in the western backdrop,

I heard something. It was like a whisper–a heavy whisper muttered in a strange language meant for my ears only. I halted on the shoulder of the highway and faced the breeze head on.

There he was. My recent research showered my imagination with a sensation of explosive bewilderment. Some fifty feet away from me, like an apparition in the knee-high prairie grass, sat a warrior upon a mighty steed, both staring at me, a look of pure rigidness on the warrior's painted face. I knew he was an older-era warrior by the distinctive battle regalia he wore. His face was painted above the nose, a slit of red streaked across his eyes while black paint covered the rest of the head above his brow. Black and white feathers adorned his head, two standing straight above his crown while four of them fluttered ghostlike in the breeze on the sides of his head. He was almost naked above the belt line, save for the hairpipe breastplate covering his chest and abdomen. In the summer sun, it hurt my eyes to look at his armour, the strips of bone so white they glowed. In his hand he held some sort of tomahawk, while the other clenched onto the horse's leather reins. A burden of fear struck me, for I did not know if this was real or a vision. I could be in danger.

For a few moments we stared at each other, the sounds of buzzing insects floating in the searing summer breeze. I didn't know what was next. I was in the middle of a foreign nowhere. Running was out of the question for there was no way I was going to beat a horse.

My mind was overburdened as I stood tall and unmoving, the summer sun searing my dehydrated skin. But thankfully, the warrior's gaze turned somewhat friendly. He nodded slowly at me without smiling, but I could still feel the kindness in his regard. His eyes then looked right past me, and I turned to face the other side of the empty highway.

As if appearing out of nowhere, there stood another man, again ancient-looking by the manner of his dress and long, braided hair. This new apparition was not a warrior. In the manner of his dress I knew he was an Elder, or perhaps a medicine man. The old man smiled, something I didn't expect. The wrinkles on his skin formed a smile which penetrated my heart with an acquainted familiarity. A familiarity that streamed through my own blood lineage.

I smiled back and even waved.

The old man, dressed in a buckskin shawl, threw his hands in the air. He started speaking softly, his enchanting voice sailing through the wind and striking my senses. It was odd but exhilarating, as the man's Blackfoot language turned all of a sudden comprehensible as though he was speaking English.

It was the deep and profound message in the Elder's words which has stuck with me to this very day. Words that I feel were for my ears and my ears only. But all I can say is that these words made me find my innermost self—the Niitsitapi that I now know was truly a part me. Just as fast as the man appeared, he was gone, driven away by the rush of a passing vehicle. The passing vehicle slowed ahead of me and pulled off onto the shoulder, politely honking its horn. I turned to where the warrior was. He was no longer there.

So, I ran to the parked truck, not wanting to make him wait.

"That thing looks heavy. Come on, you look like you can use a lift," said the driver, a lively young man who introduced himself as Dakota. I knew he was a local Blackfoot man from his accent and tanned skin. I tossed my pack into the cargo box and climbed into the truck. "Thank you so much, mate," I said, my voice a little gravelly.

He gave me a once-over before slamming on the accelerator. "What'd you camp out in the boonies or something?"

"It's a long story. And you probably wouldn't believe me if I told you," I said. "Try me," he chuckled. "I've heard 'em all."

I disclosed my full story of why I was in Canada and of the strange night I had unexpectedly encountered. The recent activity with the warrior and the Elder just minutes before had been the icing on the cake, as the old saying goes. I left out no details of the alcohol I had consumed and the tangible people I met. By the time I was done with my story, the driver slowed to a stop and stared at me, his mouth agape.

A sly grin then crossed his lips. "That old community hall. What I am about to tell you—" He paused to take a deep breath and exhale. "There was a fire there, some thirty years ago. It was supposed to be a grand celebration of two long-time lovers finally tying the knot. And then a stupid prank by one of the bride's younger brothers went wrong. The fire killed many people that night."

"Wait a minute. So, what you're saying is that I was having a merry old time…with a gathering of spirits?" My face glowed with a new understanding. Dakota glanced over at me and said, "Well, you're officially the first one–the first I know of anyway–who had that kind of encounter. And this Elder and warrior you said you just saw, just before I picked you up." His gaze became awestruck, his eyebrows raising to his forehead. "I would take that as a blessing, my friend. That means that you are accepted, that your Blackfoot bloodline runs deep within you. Never forget this moment, my friend. Never."

Dakota took me as far as I needed to go that day and as I leaned over his cargo box to grab my pack, he gifted me with a braided strand of sweetgrass.

*Alex Soop is author of two collections of short stories and novellas,* Midnight Storm Moonless Sky *and* Whistle at Night and They Will Come. *His urban home is Calgary, Alberta and his ancestral home is the Kainai (Blood) Nation of the Blackfoot Confederacy.*

## EXERCISES, CHAPTER TEN

1. Duality. "Niisitapi Reveal" is paired with *Duality* by Helena Hadala. Duality places judgement on our perception of connection and separation, our understanding of light and darkness, our feeling of stillness and movement, and the sense of self through complexities of blood lines. We belong, we exist, we encapsulate the truth of our ancestry; it resides within us and out of us. Do you have an ancestral blood line that has not been thoroughly explored for its cultural values? Drill down into this heritage and see what kind of new foods or fashion, literature or songs might emerge from this exploration.

2. Dreams. Write your dreams down. Keep a pencil and paper by the side of your bed. Use pencil because unlike most pens, a pencil will scribe when inverted. On awaking, immediately re-close your eyes, don't move. As the dream re-lights in your memory open your eyes and write it down while still lying flat. Only write for about ten seconds then re-close your eyes. Wait for dream to re-light. Repeat process until the dream disappears.

3. Synchronicity. Paxton came a long way from Manchester to Alberta to discover his ancestry and at the end of his trip he met someone who took him exactly where he needed to go. Have you kept in touch with people you've met travelling? Shoot them a note and let them know how you are doing. According to theories of synchronicity you met them for a reason. They were on your path.

*Further study:*

Castaneda, Carlos. *The Art of Dreaming.* HarperCollins, 1993

*Alex says, "Two books that made me want to be a writer"*—Taylor, Drew Hayden. *The Night Wanderer.* Annick Press, 2007.King, Stephen. *Rose Madder.* Viking, 1995.

ELEVEN

# FELINA ALOHA'S EVOLUTION

*Hilda Chasia Smith*

THE TIME I heard the sound of the gentle siren, I followed the sound and found myself face to face with an angel. It was mid-afternoon and the sun danced on the water like stars. She smiled at me and her eyes glistened blue light, her silky emerald hair shimmered, and her full, pink lips and radiant skin sent out starlight rays in all directions. Surrounded by a silvery-white mist, she floated before me, adorned in a bell-sleeved gown. Her voice, now a soft and clear siren, uplifted my heart, bringing profound tranquility. As the ocean lapped the shore and palm trees swayed, my sense of self melted away like gold under an indescribable heat.

In the angel's ethereal presence, my feminine divinity shone with an illuminating brilliance. It merged with the core of my being, revealing the true essence of who I was meant to be. Every fibre of my being resonated with a frequency unlike anything I had ever experienced. It was a symphony of soundless yet resounding harmonies, composed of sweet, flowing vowels that echoed all through my body and the very air that surrounded me. Happiness, pure and unadulterated, reverberated deeply within and around me.

In that sacred moment, I found my voice, singing like a bell, emitting a soft and melodious tone that echoed the depths of my soul. I danced with a grace that transcended the limitations of my past, embracing the divine rhythm of life itself.

Once, I had been shattered by loss and betrayal, my spirit fragmented and wounded. But the siren, with her extraordinary energy, wrapped me in an embrace that healed the deepest recesses of my being. Within me, the rising symphony of universal harmony swelled, resonating with the depths that dwell within every living soul.

Tears of gratitude and boundless bliss welled up within me, glistening like precious diamonds. Colours danced before my eyes, whispering gentle caresses upon my skin, akin to the touch of a lover. Through the enchanting call of the siren, I came to realize that this supreme energy had always been with me, an eternal presence that would forever guide and nurture my spirit. Something within me burst open—a profound awareness of this magnetic force, an invitation to embrace life's playful dance. In a hushed whisper, the angel spoke:

> Felina, I have come to remind you of your true essence, to strip away the layers of conditioning that have shaped your life since the moment you were born into this world. Your upbringing, with its teachings and experiences, has left an indelible mark upon you, but it is not the entirety of who you are. You, my dear, are a being of light and sound, a symphony of sensuality that reverberates through every fibre of your being, transcending age and time. Unblock the flow of your personal tragedy and allow the truth of your authentic self to emerge. You are more than a physical body; you are spirit, you are soul, and you are a vessel for infinite possibilities. This embodiment stretches across lifetimes, transcending the confines of a single existence. Let your light shine brightly, Felina, for you are a reflection of the boundless love and infinite possibilities that reside within you, from lifetime to lifetime.

Felina, at the age of thirty-seven, called the enchanting island of Maui her home. Born into a world of pineapple plantations and sugar cane fields, she was surrounded by hardworking people who had toiled on the land for generations. As the only child of her Hawaiian parents, Sheena and Marin, Felina's upbringing was steeped in love and a strong work ethic.

Tragedy struck Felina's life when her parents, their bellies full of liquor after attending a cousin's wedding, were involved in a devastating car accident. The weight of her grief was immeasurable, and for a year, bitter tears streamed down her face. Despite the crashing waves that echoed around her ocean-surrounded home, and the moonlight that still bathed her small blue bedroom, Felina found no solace in her pain.

In her time of need, Felina's aunt Ali, Sheena's sister, came to live with her. They had shared countless joyful moments together, cherishing the precious time spent with Felina as she grew up. Every week, Ali would join them for Sunday dinners, savouring dishes such as jerk chicken, conch, Maui onions, and crispy French fries. A delightful island salad, adorned with lettuce, pineapple, strawberries, and macadamia nuts, completed their table.

Marin, Felina's father, had been a caring and charming presence in her life, always making time for their special moments together. They would ride their bikes along the beach, take family swims, and venture out for whale watching and fishing excursions. Felina, a stunning island girl with long, flowing raven hair and deep black eyes reminiscent of lava, was only fifteen when the car accident shattered her world. The loss of both her parents left her with a profound sense of longing. It was in the aftermath of their passing that Felina discovered a hidden truth: her parents had saved and invested money for her future, ensuring she had the means to pursue higher education and forge her career.

But something had died in her when they died. She was in emotional pain for years. Aunt Ali, in her kindness, supported Felina in every possible way. Despite the grief counselor Ali found for her, Felina remained unable to unlock her emotions and discuss her feelings. She simply locked them up and drifted through the days. On the outside, a stranger would never know her truth, her sorrow. She kept it mostly to herself.

Walking along the beach in Wailea one morning, the sounds of the gentle shore bubbled with a light sea breeze that kissed her body. Felina had just graduated from university for the third time, this time with her PhD in psychology neuroscience. Exceptionally bright and addicted to studying, she had devoted herself to her studies relentlessly, earning top marks, with a very limited social life.

It was no surprise that she fell head over heels when Alexandre, a fellow student visiting from France, pursued her with kindness and charm. His handsome, tanned face and shock of brown chestnut curls, his athletic stature, and his present but not overpowering attention made her believe for the first time in years that she was healing from the tragedy of the past. She let her heart open and was allowing love to be shared.

In a romantic restaurant, Alexandre whispered Felina's name affectionately, his voice filled with emotion. "Felina, I want to marry you," he said softly, revealing a small heart-shaped ring from his shirt pocket. He brought her hand to his heart and pleaded, "Please say yes."

Tears fell like ocean pearls down Felina's face and she smiled radiantly. Soft melodies of Hawaiian music played in the background while other guests talked and laughed and enjoyed their meals, relaxing on this beautiful Hawaiian night.

"Felina," said Alexandre, "we can set up a practice together this fall. We'll make an incredible team. I want you to be my forever partner. My love for you is immeasurable." Hand in hand, they stepped away from the bustling crowd, guided by the gentle breeze. Under the embrace of the warm, fragrant air, Alexandre turned to Felina and pleaded, "Kiss me and promise that you will be mine forever."

Overwhelmed by the magnitude of her emotions Felina

surrendered to his embrace. She whispered, "Yes, my love, I am yours." After their deep kiss, Alexandre whispered, "I love you." She responded, "I love you too."

Their wedding was a small and intimate affair. Aunt Ali attended, along with a few close friends from their university days. "Oh Felina!" exclaimed Auntie Ali. "I am so happy for you, but are you sure this is the right decision? Do you truly love him?"

Felina assured her, "Yes, oh yes!"

Felina and Alexandre flew to Paris and spent their honeymoon making love morning, noon, and night, sometimes gently, with ardour, or with passion and lust in a dizzying cascade of touches, kisses, embraces, snuggles and wild abandon. They giggled and teased each other, pleased each other, and whispered dreams for the future while they basked in each other's emotions of love.

But upon their return to Maui, a shift began to occur. Alexandre's tenderness faded, replaced by demands and distance. The vibrant laughter that once echoed through their lives became a rare occurrence, overshadowed by his preoccupation with work. Felina, ever hopeful, attributed his behaviour to the pressures of establishing his practice. The long silences grew even longer, and their lovemaking came to a halt. Alexandre's words turned into venom, his actions becoming increasingly abusive.

Their lives had not been right for a long time, but it wasn't until he slapped her across the face for not purchasing the wine he desired that Felina finally made the decision to leave him for good, once and for all. So much for forever. She was heartbroken. The same hollowness in her stomach, the emptiness, and sorrow she had felt years before had intensified. She was lost and could not navigate through the turmoil.

Aunt Ali arrived at the hotel where Felina was staying and threw her arms around her niece, providing comfort as Felina sobbed and trembled like a child.

Despite Alexandre's repeated attempts to apologize for his outburst, Felina, supported by Ali, firmly stated, "We are done. Don't ever call me again." She sounded sure of herself but she felt dead inside. Again, her emotions went into hiding and she shut herself off. Felina established a small office in another building, gradually and steadily developing her psychology practice, aiding clients who, like herself, were survivors of domestic abuse.

Every day, Felina would walk by the ocean. She started to listen to nature and found it soothing. She was still locked up, but she began to tune in to herself just a little more. The songbirds seemed to be singing to her. The breezes and rain that came amidst the sunrises and sunsets were lovely sights, but still the emptiness inside was so deeply buried that even the thought of going out with someone was too much to bear.

~

*From Felina herself*

It was during that deep communion with nature that I found myself standing face to face with the angel, surrounded by her symphony of colours and sounds. It was then that I awakened to the true essence of life and learned to embrace it without fear. The angel's love and support brought an overwhelming joy, filling each breath with the confident authenticity of the divine. She whispered to me:

> We are all angels in the ethereal realm of existence. Some have received their wings but many have transformational work to do first. Felina, you are an angel with beautiful wings and a bright mind. Remain light as a feather and allow yourself to fully embody and express who you truly are—a wondrous soul radiating beauty, grace, and discernment. I see it in every breath you take. Embrace the abundance that flows within you, the miracle of your existence, and the vastness of your womanly love. Every being is deserving of complete freedom

to embrace their heavenly, natural flow on Earth and throughout the universe. Our true power does not lie in material possessions; it resides in love—the divine current that brought you to this earthly realm. Stay connected to love, for it shall guide you.

That night I made exquisite love to myself, reveling in the realization that I instinctively knew how to treat myself with tenderness and profound understanding. I surrendered to the music within, feeling the vibrant spirit of life coursing through my veins. Laughter bubbled within me, brimming with pure delight. I had once again embraced life, ready to savour each breath and every moment.

With time, I let go of my psychology practice to dedicate myself to teaching workshops on neuroscience and the behaviour of love. I could feel the angel's constant presence in the gentle breeze, the melodic songs of birds, the warm embrace of sunshine, and the symphony resonating within my heart.

At a wellbeing conference on the island of Kauai, fate brought Ricardo into my life. He was giving a seminar on the intertwined nature of intimacy and the natural world. As Ricardo began to speak, I sensed the angel's presence enveloping us both.

Later, at the reception, Ricardo stood nearby and spoke to me. "I noticed you at my seminar," he said. "Did you enjoy it?"

I replied with a smile, "Indeed, I did. It's a pleasure to meet you, Ricardo. I'm Dr. Felina Aloha, and I come from Maui. I've spent my whole life there, except for university in Oahu."

"Nice to meet you too," Ricardo responded. "What do you do?"

"I develop workshops that delve into the profound depths of love, exploring its scientific and psychological aspects for the body, mind, and soul."

I felt that my triumph over trauma must have been immediately apparent to his enlightened soul. An intense fire of divine connection wove a tapestry between us, echoing a purpose that I had never felt before As he stumbled over his words, expressing his desire to expand his consciousness and fully embrace life, I knew that the beginning of the rest of our lives was unfolding in front of us. In that moment of perfect, soulful silence, we saw and heard each other beyond words, recognizing the divine within. Sensual, sexual, intellectual, mindful, and soulful possibilities filled the air as we surrendered to the present moment, existing together as two souls basking in the genuine wonder of each other's presence.

*Hilda Chasia Smith has taught Hebrew, Yiddish, French, and English languages, charm school, music, art, meditation, and yoga. She holds degrees from The University of Calgary, The University of Manitoba, Chopra Center University, California, and Pranayama Centers International, founded by Swami Vignanananda. She is author of* Chasia's Enchantment: Meditations, Poems, Inspiration.

## EXERCISES, CHAPTER ELEVEN

1. Freedom. "Felina Aloha's Revelation" is paired with *Freedom* by Helena Hadala. In the story we see love as "true freedom of being in each moment." Look into the eyes of a beloved. Say nothing. Smile slightly. Just sit and look, really see each other for just a few vibrant, silent minutes. Smile even more deeply or hold hands in silence. What did you experience?

2. Luxuriating. Sit comfortably. Close your eyes gently. Are there any sounds or scents coming to you? Enjoy and luxuriate in them. Imagine a Lemurian crystal travelling around every part of your glorious gift of a body, radiating love in each breath as you let the flow of air move the pinkish crystal lightly and generously all over you. What is the message? Specifically, are messages of love coming to you? What gift of nature or humanity are you engaging with today?

3. Sound Sensuality. Chakra centres are connected to energy, colours, and sounds. Sound sensuality is a gateway to divine glow. It is in the voice of babies and carries through to all stages and cycles of life. Raise your vibration through compassion, passion, and love. We evolve more quickly in the truth of the beauty of who we are sensually, spiritually, and authentically. You have a physical body, a causal body, and a spiritual body. In the dance of sound sensuality, all three are at play. As you breathe, pay attention to each, singing breath, one at a time.

,

*For further study:*

Virtue, Doreen. *Angels 101: An Introduction To Connecting, Working, and Healing With The Angels.* Hay House, 2006.

Richardson, Cheryl. *The Art of Extreme Self Care: Transform Your Life One Month at a Time.* Hay House, 2009.

TWELVE

# THE MOUNTAIN, THE WIND & THE WILDFLOWERS

*Raymond Yakeleya*

THE MOUNTAIN stands before us. Not just any mountain, but Bear Rock Mountain, the special mountain of legend of my People, the Dene of the Northwest Territories. On this summer morning, my friends and I set out to climb the mountain for the first time. All my life, since I can remember, I have wanted to climb this mountain and so have my friends. Every day and in all the seasons, from our town of Tulita, we admire the mountain it in all its beauty. The day has finally come when we are old enough to cross the blue waters of the Bear River to take on the challenge of climbing Bear Rock Mountain.

My mother has told me about how she, her cousins, and her friends climbed Bear Rock Mountain when they were about my age. I have always loved her stories about how she visited two lakes on top of the mountain and a little cave. I want to see these lakes and the cave for myself, and my friends are curious too. Mother remembers the trail well enough to describe to us how to carefully walk along the face of the mountain, and then how to follow the trail upwards to the top, and beyond.

The sun is high in the sky, hot and getting hotter as we start our climb. Each of us has some canned food and water in our pack sacks. There are several tricky spots as we begin the slippery climb, but together we figure things out. The rock-strewn trail takes us higher and higher up the mountain. We are so hot that salty sweat pours off us, but we do not stop. As we climb higher and higher, we notice that we can see much further into the mountains to the west because the horizon becomes so large.

Suddenly we see an eagle's nest on the side of the mountain, all big sticks tangled up together in a big circle, as is their building style. We talk about how eagles might have soared up there for thousands of years, for maybe as long as the mountain itself. If the eagle's nest home could talk, it would tell of things that we can only imagine. We don't see the eagle but we know she is watching us.

Finally, after a very long climb, we burst onto the top of Bear Rock Mountain to a spectacular sight. The cool wind hits us, and the silence too. We do not say anything to each other at that moment, but together we observe what the eagle sees from on high—lots and lots of forests, rivers, and mountains.

For me, it is a very special feeling of accomplishment to climb the mountain, especially since it is our first time. We are all silently happy and proud of ourselves. We are sweaty, thirsty, dusty, and mosquito-bitten but in this moment we are on top of the world.

We still have another stretch of hiking to the valley of the lakes. The valley is easy to find: my mom told us to watch out for a unique structure of high rocks. The lakes, nestled in a small valley surrounded by stone walls, are a beautiful sight to behold, and we talk about how good it will feel to jump into the cold black water. Collecting a bit of firewood along the way, we make our way down to the main lake where, first of all, we take time to lay out a circle of stones and make a little fire. We respect fire as a spirit of nature so we always make sure it burns good and safe.

Once we are sure the fire is burning safely, we run down to the water's edge, tear off our clothes down to our underwear, and dive into the cold and clear black water of the lake. It feels so great! We swim and splash around for a few minutes but cannot stay in the cold water for very long. We jump out all nice and clean and gather around our small fire, shivering and chattering our teeth.

We open up our cans of beans and meat with our hunting knives, steel cutting steel, and our food is soon bubbling all over in the cans in the fire, nice and hot. We make short work of the food and it disappears in no time, except for the little bits we give back to the fire. This is our way of saying 'thank you' to the spirit of the flames for giving us its heat. Then we spread ourselves out on our towels on the ground, faces to the sun, smiling and happy.

My friends decide to take a nap, so on my own I walk along the shore to enjoy the surroundings and the silence. On the way, I notice a pink flower and lean down to look at it more closely. At that moment I notice other flowers of many different colours, scattered all over the place. I have never paid much attention to flowers before, except to pick dandelions and put them in a glass jar and bring them into the house for my mom. I draw myself even closer to the pink flower in order to smell its wild perfume. The flower is perfect in beauty and design, from its red and pink petals to its golden stamen and, of course, the glorious scent. I then look over to observe a blue flower and then a yellow one, and enjoy them in the same way. The flowers all have different shapes, sizes, colours, and perfume.

I look into the blue sky and wonder about the Creator who made the world, and these beautiful wildflowers. Who is this God the Creator, who I have heard the Elders call *Newet'sine*? I wonder this to myself and wish to know more about the mysterious being who has made these things, from the highest mountains to the smallest insect. I do not see God as I see another person, but believe with all of my heart that He exists.

I am reminded of a talk I had with my Granny Harriet one day when we walked together along the banks of Bear River, just her and me. That day, I had questioned the existence of the Creator, asking her, "Why do we never see *Newet'sine*?"

Granny answered, "My grandchild, what you are asking is good, as it means you want to learn about things that are not easy to explain. However, I will try:

> When we talk about Newet'sine, our God, we have to remember that all life comes from one place. We people love God above all things, even more than our own lives. We trust that everything happens for a reason, even though we cannot understand why things happen the way they do. The reason is often not clear until much later.

She stopped walking for a moment, briefly glanced at me, then continued, looking towards the mountains across the Bear River.

"Have you ever seen the wind?" she asked.

"No," I answered.

"Do you believe there is such a thing as the wind?"

"Yes," I replied.

"Why?" she wanted to know.

"Because I know the wind when it is on my face. When I am warm, it cools me down, and in the winter it makes me feel colder."

She turned and looked at me and smiled and said, "*Newet'sine* is like that. We can't see Him as we see each other but His spirit is in nature—the flowers, the animals, and even you and me. In all these things we can see His work, His touch, His mind, and His power. He is always with us even when we think there is no one there for us. We are made with His love and by His will. Everything is made like that. He cares for everything that He has made.

"When we do something wrong and we think we are smart because no one has seen us, it is not true. We are being watched and it is He who is watching, so we must do what is right, always. It is to Him that we must answer for all the wrong that we do.

Sometimes we make mistakes in our life, but we must always try to do what is right. We must also try to not judge people, but instead try to help when we can. This is very important, maybe the very most important thing. We must try to help everyone, especially strangers. When someone we don't know comes to our house, we always ask them if they are hungry and if they are, we feed them and give them tea. That is our way.

"I want you and all of my grandchildren to be like that. I love you all and want you to do what you want to do, but to always remember that helping people, young and old, is very important to the God who has created us. What good is it when we eat well but others have nothing to eat and suffer in life? How can we feel good about ourselves if we don't do anything when we should be helping?

> We must be kind. That is why we share, so everyone will have something. Even if it's only a little bit, it's better than nothing. Maybe it will be our turn someday to have nothing to eat and what if nobody helps us? How would that make us feel? Our people share good and bad times together. It is how we show our love to each other. We support each other in these times. It is our way.

It is as if Granny is there with me, but I look west towards the lake shore, wondering if my friends have woken up. As I walk back through the field of flowers towards our little campsite, I pick one each of the pink, blue, and yellow flowers and remember one more thing that Granny Harriet had told me.

> Our people used to die of starvation in the old days, especially in the mountains in the winter, so sharing is very important to us. We do not want to see that happen again to anyone. Many people died because of hunger when it was cold and animals were hard to get. Our Elders told us that even when that happened, our People

never blamed *Newet'sine*, but accepted what was happening. They would stand up with their last strength and face the sun and sky and thank Him for giving them the time to be alive and also to express their love for the Creator one last time. They would then fall into the snow and die with their love and belief in God. Their hearts were not hard. They were not afraid of God and of death because they knew they would be with Him and that this was part of life. It makes me so sad to think of this, my grandchild, but you have to know this and the ones following you must also know this. How many times I have said my prayers for those who suffered with no one to help them? These beliefs are part of us.

I remember that after she told me about these sad things, she turned towards me and smiled, saying,

Just because you can't see something doesn't mean it's not real, like the wind. But I want to remind you to say a prayer of gratitude every day, it never hurts to do this. Talk to God, even when you don't know what to say. Say that you want to tell Him that you love Him and want nothing for yourself. Speak with truth and honesty. He brings divine flow to your heart and your mind.

Money means nothing to *Newet'sine*. What is important to Him is what is in our hearts and our actions of what we do. I have my faith in Him always. I know that when we have a big storm with lots of black clouds, rain, wind, thunder, and lightning and when the sun is nowhere to be seen, the sun is still there, hidden maybe, but still there, like *Newet'sine*.

I am telling you these things, but look to find the truth in your life for yourself. No one can live our lives for us. Your number one rule is love God. Everything comes from that.

I look at the flowers in my hand and I silently thank *Newet'sine* for allowing me to pick a few of them, all the while thinking of my grandmother's wise words. I had made a wonderful discovery about the beauty of flowers, and all for free. *Newet'sine* is a true artist in His heart. I can see that for myself.

I walk slowly down to the shore of the lake and I can see that my friends are just now waking up from their nap. I bring the flowers to my face to smell them one last time and then throw them up into the air to scatter them onto the lake, knowing they will live longer in the water. A soft wind touches my face and hair as I watch the pink, blue and yellow flowers float away. Then, before I go back to join my friends, I bow my head.

Since it is getting late in the afternoon, we decide to go to the little cave another day. We take our time on the way back down, walking high along on the skyline, refreshed, and relaxed. The slow pace makes me think and reflect and I realize that *Newet'sine*, mysterious as always, is very real and that we are lucky to be here in this world. My cherished grandmothers have told me, "Life is precious, so let us use our time wisely."

I look across the horizon, and for a moment I thank the One who gave me my precious life and precious home. Then my friends and I look out over the steep drop of the mountain and then run down fearlessly, yelling at the top of our lungs, *"Hoo, hoo!"* We feel it is great to be alive.

*Raymond Yakeleya is an award-winning Dene television producer, director and writer. Raymond is author of the Dene children's book* The Tree by the Woodpile *and editor of the books* We Remember the Coming of the White Man *and* Indigenous Justice. *Says Raymond, "Indigenous Peoples need to have a voice in mainstream media in order to tell our stories, our way. With the passing of many of our Elders, the telling of these stories has become more important."*

## EXERCISES, CHAPTER TWELVE

1. HOME. "The Mountain, the Wind and the Wildflowers" is paired with *Home* by Helena Hadala. Home is a beautiful theme in this story with mother's home and memories of her, an eagle's nest and its soaring connection with the mountain, the vast landscape home in nature, and a divine home with *Newet'sine*. How do you identify with these various homes? Home is mother? Home is Earth and nature? Home is divine? Home is you?

2. GRANNY'S WISDOM. We trust that everything happens for a reason, even though we cannot understand why things happen the way they do. The reason is often not clear until much later. Have you ever had something happen that comes as a complete surprise? In a good way? In a bad way? Thinking back, can you accept that there might have been a lesson in the way that happened to you?

3. PAYING RESPECT. Granny's wisdom expands into love and respect for the Creator, *Newet'sine.* She says, "Just because you can't see something doesn't mean it's not real, like the wind … I want to remind you to say a prayer of gratitude every day, it never hurts to do this." Next time you take a walk in nature, pay close attention to the breath of the wind. As another way to pay respect to home and nature, silently or aloud, say a prayer of gratitude every day.

*Suggestions for further study:*

Mackesy, Charlie. *The Boy, the Mole, the Fox and the Horse.* HarperOne, 2019.

Mountain, Antoine, *Child of Morning Star.: Embers of an Ancient Dawn.* Durvile, 2022.

## THIRTEEN

# TOUGH LOVE

*Lynda Partridge*

ALIANA often felt that being a skinny young woman with short-cropped black hair made her invisible to the outside world. Since childhood she had tried to crawl into her skin to avoid being seen and to avoid being touched. She couldn't understand why the other kids called her red skin when actually she was a hue of brown. So many homes, so many escapes. So much she still didn't understand. She had cut her long silky black hair to be less visible but so far it didn't seem to help. The tattered oversized sweatshirt, weathered blue jeans and scuffed, short army boots did not achieve her desired goal of invisibility in the world.

She asked herself, *How am I still alive after all that has happened to me, all the trauma?* She knew there were lessons to be learned but for the life of her she couldn't figure them out. Bouncing from couch to couch in different people's houses trying to get a handle on things wasn't helping. As had happened before, she wondered if this was the real world for her or was the other place her actual life. It was very confusing.

She looked around the room she found herself in. It was the living room of a woman she had recently befriended—a nondescript woman whose name she'd already forgotten. *Oh yeah, that's right … this new person in my life offered me this safe spot in her apartment so I can sort things out. Whoever she is, she must have gone out.*

Aliana sighed to herself, *at least I know I'm still in the human dimension. That's a start.* She gazed around a little fearfully, but sensed that no one was present, so she curled up as small as she could, sinking into the folds of the overstuffed cushions on the couch. *Okay, I'm losing it for real this time. Gotta get outta here.* She still mumbled to herself about the discrepancies she couldn't understand. *What the heck!*

Aliana doubled herself into that familiar blanket of nothingness. Such a strange feeling each time, yet oddly comforting and familiar. She never fully controlled when she entered dreamworld, yet the path was always clear when it was about to happen. She felt comforted by the constant swoosh of warm air enveloping her. Sometimes she could hear what she felt was a soft melodic sound, an oddly familiar, comforting one. This warm swoosh sound and feeling were always her introduction to switching dimensions.

She waited for the visual evidence to show she had crossed worlds. *What will I see this time when I open my eyes?* Each time she entered the dreamworld it was a bit different than the last visit, but was always recognizable. She thought of those first visits as a young child when she had questioned what was real and what was simply a filler spot in her head to escape the atrocities of her young life. As Aliana grew older she met trusted friends who visited the dreamworld and, fortunately, taught her more about it.

Her trusted friends had explained to her that it was not the spirit world, although some people confused it with that. Instead, it was another dimension to which not everyone was able to readily travel. It was similar to going into outer space but without a spaceship or need for a spacesuit. Aliana welcomed the comfort and familiarity this dreamworld dimension provided her.

*What will you see this time when*
*you open your eyes? Shake off the human world Aliana*
*and sink into our dreamworld landscape.*

The landscape in dreamworld changed according to her age and what was happening in the human world. When she was around 5 or 6 years old, she had been a little girl in the back of a covered wagon. Whenever she crossed over into dreamworld she would be sitting in the back of the wagon travelling to some unknown destination. There were always two beings—a brother and sister sitting with her and the three of them would dangle their feet over the edge of the back end of the wagon. She was always surprised they seemed to know who she was, but she didn't know them. She always recognized their familiar smell and the design of beadwork on the hide clothing they wore. It was always the same outfit on each of them, unlike her own clothes which were always whatever she was wearing in her real human world when she crossed into the dreamworld.

The scenery was also strangely familiar, yet unknown. The ride in the wagon was always smooth but how could that have been possible in a wagon with wooden wheels, travelling on a dirt path. There were always mountains in the background that changed through different shades of purples and pinks and blues. The covered part of the wagon limited her view but staring out from behind the wagon, this is what greeted her eyes. Strangely, she had never seen any other beings, but as a child she never really made that connection. It had always brought a sense of comfort to her, something familiar and safe. It had originally been by accident that she would cross into dreamworld and it only happened when she fell asleep.

She learned at a young age to differentiate between when she was actually just dreaming and when she was crossing into the dreamworld dimension. Dreams were something most people experienced and weren't as vivid and concrete as the human world. The dreamworld dimension however was like walking through a door into another room. Nothing was distorted. You looked exactly as you did in the 'real' world. Of course the environment was purposefully manipulated to look like things that were familiar to you or that meant something to you. After all, if you crossed disembodied into the air and space of dreamworld, there was a good chance you'd lose your mind. As she became accustomed to the transfer process, she learned to have more control over when it happened.

Each time she visited dreamworld, the two beings who met her would reveal a little more about it. She came to understand that in actuality her body remained behind and that she became just spirit and soul in that dimension. The form she took was just so she didn't lose a grip on 'reality'. It was reassuring to have a body that could see and feel, as that is what she was used to in her human world. The dreamworld beings manifested in forms that she could relate to and not be afraid of, especially in her younger years. They also seemed to have a different method of tracking time. *I wonder who these beings really are? How do they see each other? Always the same or ever-shifting?* she often wondered.

She had always envisioned herself as having been kidnapped by aliens in her human world so she decided that in a way, a covered wagon was one way of being 'kidnapped'. No matter how you looked at it, the whole situation was still pretty freaking strange. Through the years, she wondered if, like in a movie she had once watched, she was actually lying in a hospital bed, restrained because she was nuts and in fact nothing was real. She had even grappled with the idea that she was dead and was just too stupid to realize it yet.

What she did learn to do was to hide this world from the other humans in the dimension where she spent most of her time. She knew that the dreamworld dimension was only accessible to a few people and once she had discovered that, she had started to embrace it.

She found that she no longer had to 'fall' asleep but that she could will herself into a sleep state while still being technically awake. It had taken years of practice but other than the time warp that happened on occasions like this time, it was a pretty seamless transfer. Aliana was hoping that by visiting dreamworld she could figure out how the time warp had happened and what she could do to correct it.

~

"Well, well, look who just couched her way in once again," Girl's voice said. "Aliana, shake off the human world. Focus on dreamworld."

"Hey, hey, Aliana where have you been?" asked Boy. We thought maybe you had deserted us."

"Yeah, yeah, I know you've just been saving up all your tough love just for me," Aliana responded groggily and somewhat sarcastically. "Seems to me last time we connected, you said I was probably a lost cause, that I didn't get it. Your humour definitely escapes me. What do you call it… dreamworld humour? Give me a couple of minutes— "

She shook her head once again. It always took a few minutes to get 'grounded' as these beings like to play little head games with her sometimes just to see if she is paying attention. I'm happy, she thought, that the covered wagon scenario ended a few years back. I never was able to wrap my head around why I would be abducted or kidnapped by 'cowboys'. Isn't it always the little white blonde-haired princess who is abducted into the savage Indian village? Why would a skinny black-haired Indian kid like me be abducted into the wagon train headed to parts unknown? Maybe this dreamworld will bring more resolve.

Whoa, whoa, politically incorrect thoughts once again. Yes it was always the Indigenous abducting the non-Indigenous into their villages and adopting them as one of their own to replace someone who for one reason or another was gone.

*So, how is the dreamworld going to look and feel this time? she wondered.* The dreamworld set had been replaced many times over depending on what was happening in her life. The only constants had been Boy and Girl in every dreamworld experience. They manifested in different ways but they were clearly always the same beings. Aliana often felt like she was switching movie sets each time she entered this world. It was a constantly moving target and sometimes the set would change while she was in it. If she became complacent about where she was, it was made abundantly clear to her just where she wasn't.

As she moved more fully into dreamworld, she said, "I can't do this anymore. I can't just keep jumping in and out of dimensions. I don't know why I can do this, and I don't know what's supposed to be happening when I do this. You keep telling me I don't belong in this world, yet every time I jump dimensions here you are. Like seriously, are you just spending your lives lurking by the door waiting for me to appear? Do you get some perverse joy in watching and listening to my scattered thoughts every time? It's been at least 15 plus years we've been doing this same dance and yet you still won't tell me why or how. Are you really the spirit world playing head games with me?

Girl's voice answered first, "We're not dead Aliana! We keep telling you we are not spirits. Quit going to séances to try and reach us through your wacky humans. And what's with you asking the Creator to make us disappear as though we're not real. Here's a news bulletin for you. It's the same Creator in all dimensions. Yeah, that's right, I said all dimensions. You seriously thought your dimension and this one are the only ones?"

Boy's voice chimed in, "Think again, girly. Glad you're here but wake up a little. It's been a lifetime, albeit so far a short lifetime, but still you're cutting into our time here. It's time for you to get it. We've gently pushed you towards understanding but you're one thick stump, you are. Think about it. You went back into your human world and you lost a huge amount of time. You don't even know where your body is in that dimension. Oh, and for the record, you're not dead and you're not restrained in a bed in some mental hospital somewhere."

Aliana gasped. "How do you even know that?"

"Well, you don't think you're the only one who can jump dimensions do you? How very egotistical of you," said Girl. "You keep coming here to dreamworld looking for answers but think about it. What answers are you looking for? What answers have you been looking for all these years? Since you were 5 years old you've been mindful of the fact that you can travel here."

Boy's voice picked up the pace: "You always blame everything on everyone around you. Yes, there are things you can't control, but there are things that you can control. Why don't you concentrate on them instead of all the other stuff? Geeze, Aliana. Its frustrating to watch in our dimension so it must be frustrating for you in your dimension and for everyone watching and listening to you. Snap your thinking head on. You're not a kid anymore. We're not going to be gentle with you anymore."

Aliana looked down at her feet and realized she was floating, and the two beings that had always looked like a brother and sister were morphing back and forth in a kaleidoscope of colour. No shape, just a fusion of colours. "What the hell. What are you two idiots doing? I'm going to vomit, if that's even possible here. Give me back a floor and plant my feet back on it. Quit using me for your personal entertainment. You've gone completely bonkers." And with that the swirling colours abruptly stopped and Aliana collided with a floor.

The colours however kept changing shape. Always two: one male one female: a priest a nun, then a rabbi and a ballerina, then a horse and a dog, then a pig and a dragon wearing a skirt, then a giant woman and a tiny man, then a tiny woman and a giant man.

"Enough already," Aliana screamed. "You have my attention." Aliana shut her eyes and slowly opened them again. This time she was sitting in a living room on a couch identical to the room in the apartment where she had started her journey into the dreamworld dimension.

Across from her, sitting in two separate armchairs were the two beings, once again manifesting as the Boy and Girl shape she was accustomed to. "So here we are. Or are we? Or where are we? Are you dreaming, Aliana? Or are you in the dreamworld or are you in your human world?" they asked in unison, taunting her. "You do know we die in this dreamworld dimension as well right? And just for the record, we'd like to see you figure out your demented lifestyle while we're still alive and breathing."

Aliana sighed and asked, "What happened to the nice comforting beings you were when I was a kid? You're more like devil apparitions now!" With that, they both transformed into cackling, clownish devils.

"Seriously you both sound like witches." The pair of them just sat there with their eyes boring into hers while they altered slowly back into their human forms.

"We're messing with you," Boy laughed

Girl asked, "Why are you here, Aliana?"

"Because you keep pulling me into your world to amuse yourselves"

"Nice try and great idea, but no," Girl said. "Think about it. When is the first time you crossed over? What was happening in your life?"

Aliana thought about it for a few minutes. She saw in her head that very first visit. She had just fallen against the huge fish tank in the family rec room in the basement and smashed the glass to smithereens. What she remembered most vividly were the goldfish all flopping and gasping for air on the carpet and someone yelling her name screaming, "What have you done?" She remembered being whisked away into the back of the covered wagon and being talked to by these two sitting across from her and wondering what the hell was going on. The flopping fish, broken glass, and water-drenched carpet disappeared. The next thing she remembered was being in a bathtub and being told to calm down and stop being hysterical. That was her very first trip into the dreamworld dimension and it was the beginning of her questioning her sanity for many years to come.

"Yeah, yeah, I remember. It was the fish incident"

Girl and Boy smiled at each other. "And why and how did

you get to us that very first time?"

"I fricking don't know. I thought I'd passed out and died."

"Think a little more."

"I suppose I wanted to disappear before I got in trouble for breaking the fish tank and those flopping dying fish were freaking me out even as a kid."

" And so...?"

"And so I disappeared, or at least I thought I did, into your world."

"Aha. And what about all the other times you've ended up here? What has made you want to cross over?"

"I suppose every time I wanted to disappear or couldn't deal with what was happening at the time."

"But remember when you crossed back that first time?" asked Boy. "You were somewhere different than where you were when you came into our dimension. You went from the floor, to our dimension, and returned to find yourself in the bathtub. You never did figure that one out did you?"

"So?"

"So you were dealing with the situation," said Boy.

"What? That doesn't make sense!"

"Aliana, whenever you come here it's always when you're in a stressful situation" Girl said. Boy nodded in agreement. "We never see you when you're in a joyful or happy situation."

"Who do you look to then, when you're happy?" asked Girl.

Aliana gave it some thought and realized she always gave thanks to the Creator when life was good. When she asked Creator for help she usually ended up in dreamworld.

"We've already told you we have the same Creator here," said Girl and Boy together.

"But you fix things for me when I come here," replied Aliana.

"No, we don't," said Girl.

"Yes, you do. I couldn't survive without this dimension."

"Yes, you can," Boy insisted.

"*No.* I can't. There's no prejudice and racism here."

"Well duh! There's also no shapes or colours," said Girl. It's not Utopia here, Aliana. You only see what Creator allows you to see."

"I'm confused. These are two different worlds?"

"Are they? Or do you just think they are?" asked Boy.

"Stop it. I know I'm in the dreamworld dimension."

"Yes, you are," said Boy. "But remember you are in both worlds. This isn't an escape route. For some reason Creator gave you the gift of visiting us here. That doesn't happen for all humans."

"Think about it, Aliana. Why are you here?" asked Girl. What are you learning? What impact will this have in your human life? It's time for you to go back to your home and figure things out."

Aliana decided that this was the worst day of her life. She couldn't figure anything out. She was hopeless.

"Just give me hint, will you?" She closed her eyes and wished everything away. There was a warm swoosh of air, and she could hear concern in their voices as she left dreamworld dimension.

*"Maybe it was too soon."*
*"Maybe we should have given her more time."*
*"What if she doesn't figure out Creator is with her everywhere?"*

The warm swoosh of air enveloped her body and carried her away from dreamworld to awaken her groggily back in human reality. Reflecting on Boy and Girl's argument and their tough love for her, allowed her to appreciate that the feeling of the dreamworld can be carried into the human world.

Aliana thinks, *I can feel the swooshing calm melodic sweet sound. This is overwhelming. Creator is with me. I don't need to travel to see Creator.* She looked around her. She saw she was still in her new friend's apartment—the new person in her life who had offered this safe spot so she could sort things out. So, there she was, still burrowed into the couch cushions.

*Everything flows between the dimensions. The human world and the dreamworld are not independent of each other.* Then, in a moment of insecurity, she thinks, *Wait, is that all I am supposed to learn?*

After a moment or two of grogginess, the realization came to her: *No matter which dimension I am in, I control nothing in it except myself. Boy and Girl have nothing to do with who I am; they are a manifestation of my trauma and they change all the time. I remain the same in both worlds. I am me. To cope, I can bridge the two worlds into one. I don't need to drift between two different worlds. I control me. I don't need to change worlds anymore. Boy, Girl, or trauma do not determine who I am; I do. I need to heal from the trauma and change me. I need nothing special. I just need to believe. I need to change too.*

Aliana was indeed still alive after all that had happened to her. She found that a way to cope with her trauma was to be visible to the world and to deal with things as they happened, one at a time. Tough love had paid off.

*Lynda Partridge is a member of the Algonquins of Pikwakanagan First Nation. She grew up in the child welfare system and spent her childhood in foster homes. While studying for her degree in Social Work, she reconnected with her birth family and with her Indigenous culture. Lynda is the author of the award-winning book* Lillian & Kokomis: The Spirit of Dance, *and* Why Are You Still Here? A Lillian Mystery.

## EXERCISES, CHAPTER THIRTEEN

1. Bridge. "Tough Love" is paired with *Bridge* by Helena Hadala. The Bridge is the safety platform that leads Aliana to assistance, help, and sharing. "I don't need to drift between two different worlds. I control me." A way to take control of your life and find your place in the world is to trust yourself and overcome limiting beliefs. Take small steps towards a goal, even if, like Aliana, you don't feel fully confident.

2. Self Healing. Go to the place in your memory you want to heal. Freeze the scene. Request a helper be in your scene, a trusted loved one. With each breath, forgive without condition and let go of any negative energy that is present. The scene could be just you in your past, or involve someone else and you in your past. Forgiveness is unconditional. Placing your hand on heart enhances security during the exercise. Continue to breathe gently and deeply. This power of self healing is not forgetting, it is remembering and accepting. Enhance the healing by sharing with a trusted friend.

3. Recovery. Asking for help is not a sign of weakness, it is a sign of strength. Trauma comes in many forms: physical symptoms like fatigue, emotional distress such as sadness and anger, problems with memory and concentration, avoidance of people, and issues with trust and intimacy. These symptoms can feel overwhelming, but here is some tough love … seek professional help with trauma specialists such a psychotherapist, psychologist, or your family doctor. These professionals are trained to help you with coping skills to overcome your trauma.

*For further study:*

Wagamese, Richard. *Embers.* Douglas & McIntyre, 2016.
Talaga, Tanya. *Seven Fallen Feathers.* House of Anansi Press, 2017.

## FOURTEEN

# ATLANTEAN ILLUMINATION

*Audrya Chancellor*

THE FIRE IS HOT and the flames dance, luminous and alluring. Entranced by the beauty and the magic that lies before her, Alleria witnesses the flames undulate.

A Wise Man sits on the other side of the fire; he seems familiar, yet she does not know him. His skin is rich and dark like soil from the earth. His white hair glistens as the fire dances, reflecting a crystalline aura field all around him. She feels the wisdom and ancient knowledge that he has within.

They do not speak. The man picks up a long wooden instrument and puts his mouth up to one end, playing a sound that Alleria has never heard before. The frequency of the sound stimulates a vibration through her entire body, making her feel heavy yet light at the same time. She feels Mother Earth's heartbeat below her, emanating love and support for her. She feels infinite gratitude towards her, as a child on the planet.

Tears well up in Alleria's emerald eyes. Her heart feels full, as her entire body connects to Mother Earth. Then, with a deep breath, she feels this loving energy become a luminous, crystalline light floating up into her feet, legs, and into her body. The man continues to play the continuous drone sound, layered with animal calls which pulse through the wooden instrument. All of a sudden, she senses rainbow spinning discs light up in her body; red discs at the base of her pelvis, orange discs in her womb, a sun illuminating in her stomach, green discs spinning at her heart, a beautiful oceanic blue disc swirling in her throat, and a glowing indigo light at her third eye, opening and softening. As the sound of the instrument grows louder and more intense, Alleria visualizes a flower blossoming on the top of her head; growing and growing. It has a thousand petals, all blossoming, dripping beautiful rainbow light down and over her fiery red hair, then her outer body. Her aura field is a rainbow—a beautiful iridescent rainbow light that extends all the way down to her toes. Alleria puts her hands to her heart with much gratitude and appreciation for this experience.

*This must be what a butterfly feels like inside its chrysalis,* Alleria thought, joyfully.

The man stops playing and looks deeply into her eyes. "The Yidaki comes from my homeland. It is sacred and healing. This is a blessing I offer you, as your people need to awaken to the Earth's changing frequency."

Alleria wakes up, still feeling the vibrations of her experience. She is lying on her bed, cozy in her room. She looks out her window and notices that everything is brighter and more colourful than usual. She reflects on her dream; she had never seen a musical instrument like the Yidaki the man played for her. It was truly a powerful experience.

~

"Alleria, are you awake?" her mother calls, entering the room. "You need to get ready for the Maiden ceremony!" Her mother, Yula, has beautiful soft, auburn hair that glistens in the light and flows down to her shoulders, framing the features on her face. Her green eyes radiate love and care.

"Alleria dear, this Maiden ceremony is very important. I told you how your father and I danced and fell in love at my first Maiden ceremony? We locked eyes across the courtyard and were magnetically drawn to each other. It is a magical experience that I know in my heart you will receive this evening. It is a very important Atlantean High Class ritual that must be honoured."

"But Mother, I had the most vivid dream! It seemed so real; as if I travelled to another land and connected with another culture. I saw patterns and colours that I've never seen before. The song of an ancient voice like Mother Earth sang through me!"

Alleria stepped out of her cozy blankets and began to get ready for the Maiden ceremony. She wondered how a dream could feel so real. *Why is my body still vibrating in such a euphoric way?*

"Alleria, you need to stop daydreaming and focus on preparing for this ceremony," her mother said. Alleria knew she was getting serious.

"Right, sorry mother. I am truly looking forward to dancing and my heart is curious if I will meet the man I will love. I heard tell that the other clans are gathering with us this evening. Young men we haven't met before!" She blushed.

"Come on then, let me help you with your gown." Yula presented the most luxurious gown that Alleria had ever been given. It was handcrafted from the finest fabric, with diamonds, emeralds, blue sapphires, and even gold-woven embroidered flowers.

"Mother, this dress is stunning! I don't mean to be ungrateful, but couldn't we use the money you invested into this dress for something more important. Like cleaning our oceans, restoring the agricultural land around the city, or helping fund a new school?"

"Nonsense my love! You are worth a fortune to your father and me. We want to support you! When you enter the Maiden Ceremony, you must catch the eyes of the right men that are in families established in the High Society and the Council. If you have dreams about helping our environment and lower classes you'll need to be a wife of someone important who can implement those decisions. Now then, please let me help you with your hair." Yula twists Alleria's strawberry blond curls into dynamic swirls with diamond and precious gems barrettes.

Alleria reflects on who she sees in the mirror and wonders: *What will become of our culture? The greed and insensitivity to nature is becoming harder for me to endure. The earth is in pain as our people continue to take without giving. Our cities are expanding into the lush, thriving forests—we are cutting down what feeds all the living beings that depend on the forest as their home. How can I truly make a difference when everyone around me is so complacent. Can I try on my own, or do I need a husband?*

Taking a deep breath and speaking aloud, Alleria makes a promise to herself. She says, "I will find a way to influence great change and soften the hearts of those who steer civilization into the lavishness that is suffocating our Mother Earth."

~

The Golden Palace shimmers as the sun illuminates the mid-autumn sky in the sweet air. The smells of delicious foods stimulate a feeling of comfort and excitement as Alleria steps into the grandiose ballroom. The bright, vibrant colours of each gown worn by the Atlantean women are exquisite. As they dance, the swirl of a beautiful palette comes to life, like a flower blossoming. The stoic and regal Atlantean men guide this collective flower with elegance and strength. Every woman is adorned with shimmering diamonds and gems that sparkle and illuminate the room. Alleria is whisked into the energy, finding herself in the hands of a man she does not recognize.

"My dear sweet lady, may I have this dance?" His voice serenades her. "I am Zoddok, son of Orion of the High Council. We are visiting from Laratice, beyond the mountains and enchanted forest." Zoddok stands tall with broad shoulders, strong, and very handsome. His golden hair shines like the sun and his blue eyes are deep like the ocean. His smile and charisma could melt anyone's heart.

"I am Alleria from the Atlantean city, Vaclitia. It would be my honour to dance with you," she replies.

Soon they are dancing and weaving within the collective radiant flower of fabric, laughter, and joy. Alleria's shimmering gown drapes on her beautiful body, flowing with the music. The sounds of each instrument harmonize to create the perfect atmosphere for this ceremony and celebration.

Zoddok gazes into Alleria's emerald-green eyes. Entranced, he says, "I feel like I'm floating in a dream with you. Forgive me for being so forward, but you are the most beautiful woman I've ever encountered."

Blushing, Alleria responds, "You are too kind, but are you also interested in knowing my heart's desires for our people and the future of our world? Do you fancy a woman who can speak her truth and not be lured away by wealth and opulence?"

As they dance Alleria looks carefully at Zoddok to gauge his response. "Forgive me for being so forward, but what is this High Class ritual really for when people are starving and our earth is suffering? Have you thought about these injustices or are you blinded like everyone around us?"

Zoddok had actually not ever given any thought to these things. He feels his heart become heavy from hearing these truths and he knows that something must change in order for balance to be restored. He also feels hope in his heart that he can right these wrongs, as his father sits on the High Council. He wonders if his father would listen to him; he knows this woman speaks from her heart and feels a great change about to happen.

Suddenly, as Alleria and Zoddok spin and whirl, they feel the floor shake and shift under their feet. The collective dancing flower begins to break apart into fractured petals as each couple staggers from the dance floor, terrified by the instability they are experiencing. The floor cracks open and screams echo through the ballroom.

Alleria and Zoddok hold each other tight as they seek out a place of safety from the chaos. They run towards an archway that looks out over the city. Below, they see townspeople panicking in the streets as monuments, statues, and works of art crumble to the ground. They grab onto marble pillars to find stability as the ground shakes more violently.

A great fissure in the ground opens between Zoddok and Alleria, causing Zoddok to lose his footing and slip into the void opening beneath them.

"Zoddok!" She screams as she reaches out for him. Zoddok slides down the shattered marble floor, unable to clutch onto anything secure.

"Alleriaaaaa!" His voice is distant, then vanishes.

Atlanteans are in utter panic and confusion. Alleria closes her eyes and sees a flash of the Wise Man from her dream. "Alleria remember you have the energy within you to help your people as the Earth's frequency changes." She opens her eyes and wonders aloud, "What does that even mean? My world is being torn apart all around me. How can I help anyone right now?"

In the distance, a huge wave rushes in with a force of destruction and chaos. The earth cracks open even wider and the city collapses down into a dark abyss as the water rises, transforming the landscape into a watery grave.

Screams pierce Alleria's heart, yet she remains speechless as she witnesses the collapse of everything she ever knew. As the Golden Palace sinks, she holds onto the pillar with all her might, even as the waves rush up all around her. She takes a deep breath, possibly her last, and then everything disappears.

~

A melodic song captures Alleria's attention. Somehow, she is lying in a cave with crystals glowing all around her. Her body aches and she sees her own blood dripping onto a cave floor. Too weak to stand, Alleria rests her head on a smooth stone. The singing becomes louder as an elegant woman appears from the depths of the cave. Her hair is silver, like the crystals. Her eyes are lavender; kind and gentle. Alleria feels calm and relaxed in her presence.

"My dear sweet child, how are you feeling? My name is Saraphine and you found your way to my hidden home beneath the great Atlantean city of Vaclitia. No one has ever visited me and now here you are, just as I had dreamed you would come. Please, let me help you with your wounds and nourish you while you regain your strength."

"How did I get here? The last thing I remember is my entire city being destroyed and water rushing up over top of me. What happened to my people, my family, my friends?" she begins to cry, tears streaming down her soft cheeks. Her heart is shattered and an immense pain surges through her body.

Saraphine begins to sing again, taking deep breaths and holding out her hands towards Alleria's heart. Alleria welcomes her soft nurturing touch as the tears continue to rain down and her body heaves with sorrow. Saraphine's hands are warm and comforting; Alleria feels tingles of energy enter her heart, calming her body. She breathes deeply with Saraphine and a calming relaxation flows over her entire body. The crystals begin to light up as the beautiful song continues. Glowing brighter, they begin to move. They levitate into a mandala design that swirls all around Alleria; resting above her head, sending ripples of healing energy down through her crown, illuminating her body with white and golden light. She feels the colourful spinning disks activate in her body the same way they did in her dream when the Wise Man played his Yidaki.

Alleria feels this song harmonizing in her soul and begins to sing with Saraphine. Her body awakens to a new vibrational human experience. As they sing together, their voices weave and create a sparkling energy that Alleria can see, this energy swirls around them, connecting their hearts. Alleria feels so much love that her body becomes devoid of any pain and discomfort. She is as light as a feather and almost loses the sensation that she has a body. It is as though her body becomes one with the song, becomes one with the crystals around her, becomes one with Saraphine, and becomes one with the moment. She looks down to see her wounds are healed and she feels a rush of energy tingling all over her. She begins to see her aura field again, illuminated with a multicoloured, iridescent glow.

Energetic wings sprout out of her back and she flexes her upper back, flapping these wings open to take flight. Her body begins to lift off from the crystal cave floor as she rises up towards the entrance of the cave. Saraphine continues to sing and Alleria's heart fills with so much joy and radiance that her wings flutter faster. She finds herself leaving this magical experience behind, yet is still encapsulated in a rainbow chrysalis as she begins her journey through the maze of crystals towards a light. Rising closer and closer to the opening, the light fills her emerald eyes with hope, vibrancy, and purpose. Alleria rises up through the rocky mouth of the mountain cave into the bright, warming sunlight.

Floating above where her beloved city once stood, she is shocked to see water has taken over. The destroyed remains are now underwater, lost to the splash of waves that lap up along the edges of the mountains, which circle the city that once stood in grandeur.

"How could this have happened? Where is everyone?" She shouts. Her wings stop fluttering, catapulting her down to the earth. She tumbles on the rocks and lands in the water with a large splash.

Alleria is an excellent swimmer and at that moment decides, "I need to look for my loved ones! Any survivors!" She swims with all her might and tears well up in her eyes at the sight of her home that is completely demolished. Strange, though, that amongst all the rubble there isn't a single body. Not a trace of her people.

"What happened to everyone?" Alleria calls out as she continues to search, knowing deep in her heart she has to find answers.

The sun is setting and she is exhausted. Alleria swims towards a forest on a hill that is still being illuminated by the setting sun. Hungry, cold, and hopeless, she reaches the shore and pulls herself out of the water onto the earth and curls up to a tree, still in disbelief that any of this is real.

"I'm going to wake up and this will all be a dream! It just has to be, this doesn't make sense." She is too exhausted to walk so she embraces herself in the warmth of her luminous wings, falling asleep next to a large oak tree. The tree gives her comfort and a sense of connection, as if it is hugging her. She breathes in the tree's life force and love. As she breathes out, the pain she feels at the loss of her family, her friends, her community, her home are absorbed by the tree.

~

A wet sensation laps on Alleria's face as she slowly opens her eyes to discover a small golden fox licking her. Alleria giggles as she reaches out to see if the fox is real. The fox looks at her with mystical, diamond-blue eyes. Alleria strokes the golden fur, feeling a sense of magical bliss and comfort. The fox is snuggly and makes adorable chirping sounds.

"Why hello sweet little fox! Where did you come from?" The fox begins to prance around Alleria, influencing her to stand up from her grassy bed next to the tree. Stretching her arms up high, she feels the tree's presence again, "Thank you, magnificent tree, for absorbing my pain while I slept. I feel well rested and ready to find answers today. Little fox, would you like to come with me on a journey? I don't know where I'm going, but I would love to have your company." The fox dances around her with joy and begins to walk along a path with silver and purple flowers, into an Enchanted Forest. "I guess I'll follow you as I'm sure you know your way through this forest," Alleria says.

Alleria had always been warned by her mother and elders not to venture into the forest surrounding the city. She remembers her mother saying, "Alleria, it is dangerous. Any time one of our clan members ventures into that forest, they never return."

The fox brings Alleria to a bush of golden berries and trees filled with golden pears and golden apples. She is excited as it feels like days since she has eaten. "Perhaps it actually has been days since I've eaten!" Time was becoming a blur but in this moment she gives gratitude for this nourishment. "Thank you so much little fox for bringing me here! Thank you golden berry bushes, and thank you trees. This is the most delicious fruit I've ever tasted."

The fox chirps again and dances around Alleria's feet. Feeling completely satiated, Alleria bends down to stroke the fox's fur. Her beautiful, shimmering wings open up again and pulse. "The joy in my heart must activate my wings," Alleria says. The fox gives her a curious look, then begins to bark loudly and jumps around her, startled. "What is it, little fox? Are my wings upsetting you?" Then he runs away. "Come back friend!"

Alleria hears a loud snap in the forest and a hidden net falls from the trees and encapsulates her. "Help! Little fox, come back!" Panicking, Alleria's wings get tangled in the netting and she is bound into stillness as the net tightens around her and she falls to the ground.

Four rugged, yet handsome Elves emerge to observe their prey. Surprised to see a beautiful Atlantean maiden, they turn away to talk amongst themselves. Alleria can hear their Elven language being spoken, but she doesn't know what they are saying. It seems that they are in a disagreement. Two of the Elves approach her and begin to cut the net to set her free, but then bind her hands and lead her deeper into the Enchanted Forest.

"Where are you taking me?" She asks, even though she is uncertain they can understand her. They don't say anything. The silence is a tangible. The two Elves who tied her up seem quite clear that she is their prisoner, their prey, their trophy. The other two Elves walk behind her and Alleria can sense their uncertainty and curiosity.

Alleria had been told stories of an Elven race that lived deep in the woods and who were not welcome in the Atlantean cities. There was a great war between the Elves and Atlanteans many moons ago, long before Alleria was conceived. The Atlanteans drove the Elves deep into the forest, taking the land that was by the ocean and beyond the mountains. The Atlanteans feared the Elven ways of magic and mysticism. Above all, Atlanteans believed in science and technology, grand architecture, statuary, and logic.

As they venture through the forest, they step over huge roots, passing trees that become larger and grander the further they travel. They cross pristine, clear creeks and finally come to the mouth of a cave in a large mountain. Alleria looks up, but she cannot see the top of the massive rock face. The Elves pull her inside the cave and as Alleria's eyes adjust slowly to the dimness, her heart begins to beat rapidly and she is inspired to sing. Her song echoes through the cave, sounding like multiple beautiful angels singing in a choir. The Elves stop in their tracks. The song is familiar to them.

The caves begin to glow and shimmer like magic amethyst all around them. The song she sings is the one that the wise woman, Seraphine, taught her. The Elves stare at each other in astonishment. How could she know their Mage song? Instead of taking Alleria down into the depths of their dungeon, they escort her to the King and Queen of the Elves.

They walk for hours, deep into the crystal cave, passing by other Elves. Women and children look curiously at this outsider. Other Elvens stop their work to stare in awe at this unfamiliar, radiant maiden. A procession of Elves begin to follow them as they approach the throne room of the King and Queen. At the golden doors of their throne room stand two large guardian Elves that question the arrival of this young woman. After a long conversation which Alleria wished she could understand, one of the Elves opens the door and ventures to request an audience with the King and Queen.

*What will they do with me?* Alleria wonders. *Why have they all gathered behind us to witness my capture? They look curious and intrigued. It must have been centuries since they have seen an Atlantean, let alone one in their crystal caves.*

Finally, the Elves come back and open the doors wide for Alleria to enter with her escorts. The procession of Elves waits outside and are encouraged to go back to their daily tasks. Alleria is astonished to see such beauty and luminous light in the throne room. The Queen's energy and presence is so powerful that tears well up in Alleria's eyes and she feels her heart expand with love. Her wings begin to flutter again, gently as she walks toward the royal couple. The Elves are mesmerized by Alleria's wings, her elegance, and regal grace. The King looks upon her with a deep knowing, as if he recognizes Alleria.

"What is your name, child, and why have you come to the Enchanted Forest?" Alleria is shocked to hear this question in her mind and heart. Not a word is spoken out loud, but she hears the voice clearly. She uses her inner voice, her thoughts, to send a message to the King and Queen.

"I am Alleria from the Atlantean city which was once Vaclitia. My home has been destroyed and my people have disappeared. Do you know what happened above these caves? What happened to my people, my family, my loved ones?" Alleria was doing her best to hold back her tears.

Alleria heard the King's and Queen's unspoken words, "We have seen visions of this destruction, this cleansing. Centuries ago, the Atlanteans took our homes and drove our people deep into the Forest. We chose to live peacefully within the mountain and thrive with nurturing from the earth. Watching from afar as your people continued to take from the earth not giving back, creating monumental structures that tower in the sky as if reaching towards the heavens to find a connection with the cosmos above, yet honouring neither the cycles of the earth nor the star nations. Atlanteans focused on technology, science, logic and did not listen to the deeper rhythms of their hearts and the heart of our Mother

Earth, our earth that nourishes us, gives life and connects all living things."

Their regal message continued, "Your people disregarded these ways, manipulated the natural order and brought pain and suffering to the earth through what they considered cultural advancement. The earth grew tired of the destruction of her forests, animals, all living creatures that breathed the sour air that was created by Atlantean industrialization. Earth chose to regenerate and wash clean the burden that was bringing pain and suffering. Your people are gone and their souls are lost in the great void."

Alleria does her best to digest this information, but she is in disbelief. She thinks of her mother, Yula, her father, Promoxis, and her heart connection with Zoddok. Her people were kind. True, they loved their lavishness, technology, and advancement of science. The cities continued to grow each year as the forests were cut all around them to make space for the new development. There was a thick smog in the air that became dense when the winds were calm. Alleria loved her days by the ocean as the breeze would clear the air and she could frolic in the waves. There weren't many spaces like that in her city and she had always longed to venture into the forbidden forests.

Alleria responds, "How do you know this to be true? Why am I still here? Why wasn't I swallowed up by the waves that took my people?"

Just then the Wise Mage Saraphine appears in the throne room. Her presence brings peace and delight to Alleria and she takes a deep breath, replying to Alleria's questions, "Because my dear sweet child, you are the one who will help your people ascend from the Great Void. You have a heart that is connected to Mother Earth and you have a gift within you to heal the wounds of the ancestors. Use your voice and sing with me."

Saraphine begins to sing and the crystals in the cave glow; the energy of the song swirls in Alleria's heart as she joins in this euphoric experience. Once again, she feels rainbow discs spinning in her body, a fountain of energy flowing through her and around her. Alleria's wings open and flutter as she rises above the ground and begins to dance in the air. She is surprised to see her loved ones, her people, all around her. They are faint, grey forms of light that echo each individual she has ever known, and others who she knows are Atlantean, but hasn't met. They all reach out to her, yearning for help.

Alleria sings louder and pulses her wings faster, focusing on the rainbow light that is radiating from her body. She anchors this light with Mother Earth's heart centre sending it deep down into her core. She illuminates her light up through the top of her head, sending it up towards the sky, through the atmosphere and into space anchoring with a star, her guiding star above. With a deep breath, while she and Saraphine continue to sing, Alleria draws strength and energy from Mother Earth and her Guiding Star into her heart and begins to glow a golden sphere around her body which expands to fill the entire throne room, washing over each one of the lost souls. Her ancestors, her loved ones, her people begin to vibrate with this golden light and ascend towards the guiding star above. Each one bows in respect, gratitude and love for Alleria and her ability to assist them through their transition out of the Void and into the nurturing light. The last Atlanteans Alleria witnesses are her Mother, her Father, and Zoddok as they come closer to embrace her with their love. Alleria's tears continue to pour down her face and she knows this is their fate and that they will be at peace. Together they say, "We love and appreciate you so much Alleria." She hears this in her heart as they vanish into golden light.

*Audrya Chancellor has been offering Reiki and Sound Healing internationally for over twenty years. She has a passion for assisting people to connect deeply with their hearts and supporting them to illuminate from within. This is her first published story and she is inspired to continue writing. Audrya lives in Mendocino, California.*

## EXERCISES, CHAPTER FOURTEEN

1. Delight. "Atlantean Illumination" is paired with *Delight* by Helena Hadala. Delight in this story coincides with Alleria's expected or unexpected sensation of peace and ecstasy, floating in the protection of love. What has delighted you lately; something that has given you a sense of great pleasure, joy, or happiness? Is this something worth repeating tomorrow, or the next day, or is it something rare and unusual? Can you create this feeling of delight in other ways?

2. The Yidaki: Didgeridoo. Sonic frequencies fundamental to the sound of the didgeridoo are in the low-frequency range of 60 Hz to 200 Hz. To successfully achieve these sounds on the didgeridoo, circular breathing is required. Inhale deeply through your nose and fill your lungs with air. Then fill your cheeks with air, pucker your lips and create a small opening for the air from your cheeks too escape from your mouth. As you push the air out of your mouth using your cheeks, simultaneously inhale through your nose. When your cheeks are empty, exhale air from your lungs through your mouth to continue producing sound.

3. Mother Earth. In the story, Alleria is told, "You have a heart that is connected to Mother Earth and you have a gift within you to heal the wounds of the ancestors." The Atlantean wounds included destruction of the forest and its living creatures and the thick smog. Alleria was urged to "use your voice" and take action. How do you use your voice to take action against lavishness and pollution to help heal the Earth?

*Further study:*

Redfield, James. *The Celestine Prophecy.* Warner Books, 1993.

Medicine Eagle, Brooke. *The Last Ghost Dance: A Guide for Earth Mages.* Bear & Company, 2000.

FIFTEEN

# THE SACRED PLACES STORIES TAKE US

*Iikiinayookaa Marlene Yellow Horn*

OKI IITAAMMIKSKAANAATONI, hello and happy day! I write this chapter from a place of anticipation, excitement, and great humility. Nitanikowa, I am Iikiinayookaa Marlene Yellow Horn, and I am the mother of Saapaata Wacey Rabbit and daughter-in-law Ashley Callingbull-Rabbit, wife to I'tsaapoyi, Marvin, daughter of Patsy and Larry Rabbit, a sister, a granddaughter whose grandparents are from the Rabbit, Goodstriker, Soop, and Blackplume clans. I am a daughter, sister and granddaughter of residential school survivors. Here, I share with you Blackfoot stories of sacred places and acts, hoping you will find a connection to build relational links and trust. Furthermore, you may be able to reflect on my words to cherish the wisdom of your own ancestors' stories, to take care of each other, as the animals did at Oohkotok, and to face your challenges head-on, like the buffalo.

I spent my formative years at the heels of my grandmothers, mother, and aunties. I loved hearing the stories and laughter, as well as feel the strength from the women who gave me character and made me inquisitive, forever searching for reasons and answers. Each woman in my circle afforded me a worldview unfaltering in mookaakiit iikaitkiimaat, perseverance, persistence, commitment, resilience, and a never-ending view of moving forward. Each teaching taught me the values of my People, the Kainaiwa of the Blackfoot Confederacy.

Stoney Nakoda Elder Henry Holloway reminds us that a story is like a blade of grass. The base of the blade of grass is its foundation—where the truthfulness of the story resides. We all share our stories differently: some are so theatrical in their storytelling that their hands, facial expressions, and voice tones are appendages of the story, releasing like an erupting volcano. Others share stories in a reserved fashion, keeping their hands close to their body; their facial expressions modest, so as to release the story like a babbling brook, to build anticipation and suspense. Then again, some share their gift of storytelling, like the rising and falling of the ocean tide, eruption at the height of the wave, and then the calmness of a mid-summer night breeze, the slow release of details to weave a memorable story. It does not matter how a story is shared; all that matters is the truthfulness of the story; the foundation is all that remains.

Blackfoot creation stories have been told since time immemorial, sharing our ways of being, knowing, and belonging on this land they call Siksikaitsitapi, the original people of the land. Each creation story shares how the Blackfoot people conduct themselves with the land and each other, how to sustain themselves, providing all they need to lead a successful and good life. Napii, our Blackfoot trickster, provides entertaining and comical scenarios which also offer lessons in humorous and exciting adventures. His connection with the animate and inanimate world provides a glimpse into the holistic worldview connections of the Blackfoot people.

The story of Oohkotok, the Okotoks Big Rock Erratic, is a story of what the Blackfoot People of this territory believe about a huge rock that tumbled far from the Rocky Mountains. Yes, Western science has its interpretation based on proven scientific theories, however, Siksikaitsitapi People believe the story of Oohkotok originated from the lessons provided by our Blackfoot trickster, Napii.

Napii was a tall, handsome, and adventurous man who always found himself in tricky situations, along with his best mate, Coyote. Many relatives shared the story of Napii and Oohkotok throughout my childhood. Each storyteller shared the story uniquely, always ensuring the truth remained at the base of the blade of grass.

Nestle in, make yourself comfortable, and travel with me thousands of years ago to a time when Napii walked freely and could communicate with all that was alive with energy: the animate and inanimate beings of this territory.

~

Napii was traveling North with his buddy Coyote, carrying a buffalo robe for warmth on this day. The day began beautifully with a bright sunrise to the East and a calm breeze from the West, and as the day progressed, the sun rose in the sky, making for a beautifully clear and hot day. Along the way, Napii told funny stories of his many adventures to his buddy, Coyote. Often you would see Coyote glance and roll his eyes when Napii's stories began to tread into the many troubles he found himself in. You would also see Coyote shake his head as he remembered how he helped Napii escape safely from these same hazards.

Napii decided it was time to rest. He was tired from carrying a heavy buffalo robe in the hot sun, which made his travel very difficult. He and Coyote came upon Oohkotok and they decided this would be the best place to rest and find shade from the hot sun. Coyote helped Napii lay out the buffalo robe and Napii continued telling his many stories.

After a while, Napii decided to continue north on the journey. He told Coyote that the buffalo robe was too heavy to carry on this hot day and he would leave it behind. Coyote did not think this was a good idea—the cool air of evening would arrive, and Napii would need the robe for warmth. Besides that, Coyote knew that a storm was coming from the West and that Napii would regret his decision. Napii hastily turned to Oohkotok and thanked him for providing shade and a place to rest. In his appreciation, he offered Oohkotok the buffalo robe. Oohkotok was happy to receive such a precious gift and expressed his gratitude.

The journey continued, and as predicted by Coyote, the storm quickly rolled in, bringing strong winds, rain, and sleet of wet snow. The temperature soon dropped, and Napii quickly regretted his decision to leave the buffalo robe behind. As Napii wrapped his arms around himself, leaning into the wind with his head cast down, he looked at Coyote and asked him to return to the Oohkotok rock to get his buffalo robe back. Coyote declined many times, knowing it was not right to take a gift back, and he, too, was cold and did not want to run all the way back to Oohkotok. Napii eventually convinced the reluctant Coyote to return to the big rock. Upon his arrival at Oohkotok, Coyote first asked for the robe back, but Oohkotok refused the request. So, Coyote returned to Napii, but Napii rebuffed and told Coyote to go back again and take the robe without asking. Coyote knew better than to argue with Napii, so he went back and took the robe back without asking.

As they continued their journey, Napii wrapped himself in the warmth of the newly returned buffalo robe. Coyote was mad and refused to listen to his friend as he resumed the many stories he had to share. The storm continued, but Napii and Coyote noticed a huge ominous sound accompanying the shower, and then they noticed the ground was vibrating as well. At the same time, the friends looked behind and saw big rock Oohkotok angrily rumbling toward them at great speed. Napii and Coyote knew they were in a mess of trouble and needed to stop Oohkotok before they were run over.

Napii called out to the animals of the prairies for help. At first, none of the animals would help; however, after much pleading, the animals began to help one by one. The beavers arrived, but the rock ran over their tails, so that is why beavers have flat tails. Next, the gophers came. At this time, they were large human-like animals and Napii hoped their strength and size would stop Oohkotok, but this was not meant to be. The giant gophers were run over and squished into a small hole; therefore, gophers are now small animals who make their homes in the earth along the prairies. A flock of sparrows subsequently arrived and decided that they would fart on the rock to slow it down; however, the farts turned to poop that plastered the rock, which is why green lichen can be found on Oohkotok today.

By this time, Napii and Coyote thought their days were numbered as Oohkotok's rumbling turned into crashing, inching closer and closer to them. Finally, the bats arrived and began using their large beaks in unison, pecking at Oohkotok. Slowly Oohkotok started breaking apart and come to its modern-day resting home in southern Alberta, but not before the bats' beaks were diminished in size as we know it today. As in the past, the prairie animals saved the day and saved Napii from catastrophic demise.

Each Napii story is intended to teach a life lesson and is part of our creation stories. This story shares how the animals' physical features came to be and how Oohkotok came many miles from the Rockies to a rolling valley outside Okotoks. As a child, my immediate lesson was not to take gifts back; however, as I got older, I reflected on the importance of living in a community and being compassionate by taking care of each other, as the animals did on this day. I also reflected that although Napii found himself in trouble, his good intention of sharing his buffalo robe with the Oohkotok was an act of reciprocity, which continues to be a value practiced by Siksikaitsitapi.

I'm sitting in church on a hard bench, waiting for my mom, who speaks in a hushed tone to another lady at the back of the church. I wear a pink dress, straw hat, white socks with lace, and shiny black shoes. As I look at my shoes, I realize how uncomfortable my feet feel. I don't understand why I can't wear my boots to church. At almost this same time, I look around the church, and the thought enters my mind, "I don't belong here; this is not for me." I am 6 years old.

~

I have always loved to read. I remember the library was my favourite place in the school. I treasured the moments when I could run my fingers across the bindings of the shelf-filed books, imagining where the stories could take me in my mind and where the characters became my friends. I held books in high regard and would often share my keen appreciation for literature with my mom. Before I board my flight to Providence, Rhode Island, I purchase a book at the airport, *Marley & Me*, written by John Grogan. The book is written from the family dog's perspective; this is so exciting and reminds me of our dog, Scout. The story entertains me and makes me laugh, and I become very fond of the many adventures of Marley and her perspective. In Providence, I will soon be visiting my son, Saapaata, who has moved across the continent to play hockey. I explore the city of Providence, alone at first. I see the building where the original *Ghost Busters* movie was filmed, eat a stuffed-shrimp dinner, and walk along the waterfront enjoying the historic water fire sculpture, with the book as my companion.

~

I am five years old and excited to help with morning chores at the barn with my brothers and dad. As I walk outside our front door, I am struck with the beauty of the rising sun and then the fresh crispness of the morning air. The smell of manure and wet dirt creates a reminder of what is to come for many years. My dad always begins with the statement, almost a declaration, "We take care of our animals before we take care of ourselves." He goes on to share that animals give of themselves to make our world brighter and safer—in our case, the horses allow us to live the life of rodeo and our cows allow us to make a good living. I wonder, is he just referring to our animals or all animals? This question would be answered by my grandparents when teaching the importance of reciprocity and respect. I stay behind while the others go inside for breakfast. I remember looking to the East and seeing the beautiful grass; what I would learn later is called prairie wool, what seemed the unending, unobstructed view of Old Agency. It is here, at this moment, when I first begin to ask the question, who was here before me? This query never leaves me; I remember riding my horse to help chase the cattle in, riding my horse to the river bottom, riding my horse while picking berries, and finally, riding my horse to travel to our neighbours to visit—thinking, and imagining those who walked and rode the same path before me.

~

It is 2010, and for 24 years, I have been the mom of a strong, handsome, well-travelled young man. On my last day in Oslo, my son Saapaata and I went sightseeing and shopping. When we left the loft, he turned to me and said, "Put a hat on; it's cold out there." As we started our journey, it began to rain, drizzling to clean the air, then large raindrops from heaven. He went into a store and, without a word, bought me an umbrella, saying, "Here, I don't want you to get wet." As the rain continued, my Ugg boots began to get soaked, so he walked into a store, saying, "Pick a pair of boots. I don't want your feet to get cold, and you go home sick." Lunch was delicious, and the conversation was filled with laughter and words to make me feel okay with my son being so far from home. As we walked through the streets of Oslo and by the pier, he would gently take my elbow so I would not slip and slow my walk, "Mom, you need to slow down; Europe is all about enjoying life, not running through it." We ended our excursion with delicious café au lait in a small coffee shop. We sat by the window in silence, both with our own thoughts. It was then that I realized my son was indeed a man. A man with wise words to share with his Mama, a gentle hand to help me along, and a man who understands the importance of family. The tide of life had quietly turned, and it was then I knew my son would be fine in this world.

~

I am excited for my first day of school. My big brothers are just as excited for me to go too. The bus travels up our road, and my mom grabs brown paper bags for my brothers and me. She looks at my feet and immediately takes my cowboy boots off my feet. As I resist, she hurriedly puts on the shiny black shoes. I am mad. I am embarrassed to wear the shoes to school. I resist. As my mom drags me to the bus, she is mad at me because she does not want me to miss the bus or for her to be late for work. I refuse to get on the bus; I remember Mrs. Lilly, the bus driver, smiling and reminding my mom that the type of shoes I wear are unimportant. As I sit on the bus, looking at my cowboy boots, I realize I have a voice. I arrived on my first day of school on time wearing my cowboy boots, which I wore every day to school.

~

It has been precisely 11 years and 4 months since I have dwelled on this earth without my parents. It seems that I have survived my life just living, hoping to one day be alive again. I stand on the sandy beach of the Sea of Japan on this cold cloud-covered December afternoon. I close my eyes and inhale the saltwater breeze while listening to the crashing waves. And in a moment, I feel my feet begin to move, forward then backward, I open my eyes, and I find myself playing with the tide. I laugh; I feel the coolness as I take a breath, which reminds me of the smile that has evaded me since my dad took his last breath. I feel laughter in my chest before I hear it. I stop and look back at Saapaata, my son, who is filming me, and when I return my gaze to the sea, I feel my spirit return to me, and I feel whole again. I have lived until I feel alive.

Elders remind children always to show characteristics of the buffalo. The buffalo is a strong, stoic, and fierce animal of the prairies, the only animal who will walk directly into a storm while the other prairie animals turn their backs to the storm to seek warmth. By stepping into the storm, the buffalo is the first to move out of the stormy weather and eat the grass on the other side. The storm in this story is a metaphor for the challenges or problems humans face. If you humans face your challenges, then resolution, safety, and security will be met and not prolonged by avoiding the problem. Always show the character of a buffalo.

As a child, my mom shared that my grandparents marked my wealth in grandparents. When I was born, I had nine living grandparents on both my maternal and paternal sides. I never really understood the connection between wealth and grandparents. When I was a child, my grandpa Frank Goodstriker would begin all his stories with, "Twenty years ago…" This declaration changed around the arrival of my son; you knew a good story was going to be shared when you heard, "Forty years ago…" Grandpa was a wrangler for the Blood

Band Ranch when he was a young man and father. He shared that one day after a snowstorm in February, he and another wrangler made their way across the prairies to gather cattle. The snow was knee-horse deep, making travel difficult, and the combination of sunshine and wind caused the snow to reflect brightly. As he travelled, he and his friend shared stories, sang Blackfoot songs, and laughed. My grandpa didn't realize the problem until his friend asked if he was okay; my grandpa began to steer his horse in the wrong direction. It was then he realized he was snowblind. Much to my horror, I began to ask why he didn't wear sunglasses, did he go to the doctor, and how long he had been snowblind. All my questions were met with laughter and a hug to comfort me; I was always the first of the grandchildren to ask questions. My grandpa made his journey to the Sandhills 33 years ago this summer. When I hear the song "Grandpa Tell Me About the Good Old Days" on the radio, I am reminded of my wealth.

Elder Narcisse Blood reminds us that we are born Niisitapi; however, we spend our whole lives becoming Niisitapi. It is stories that have filled and fueled my spirit. Stories, thousands of years old, told by many generations, have taught me my place, role within my family and community, and who I am as a Siksikaitsitapi woman. And I realize that my stories and our creation stories take me to sacred places in becoming Niitsitapi.

Although I did not attend residential school, please know that I experienced all the effects of the generational trauma passed from five generations. My parents attempted to shield me from the horror of their stories; however, the effects found me in the small crevices of my existence. I didn't know why, but I instinctively knew that this was not what life should be and what life could be for my family and me.

My beautiful mother taught me that we were a collective, a family and that we were to love and accept everyone with compassion. She taught me not to question why my aunt chose to spend ten years of her life lost to addiction on the streets of

East Hastings without her four children, but to love her anyway in her absence and presence. And, why today, I drive the streets of Calgary in the wintertime looking for my cousins to bring them food and warm clothing and, in the summertime, water to keep them cool. I claim the blood that runs through all my relations and it is here that I experience a divine flow of love in this sacred act of bringing comfort to my People.

*Iikiinayookaa Marlene Yellow Horn is a Blackfoot author and educator from the Mamoyiksi Fish Eater Clan of the Kainai First Nation. Iikiinayookaa received her Master of Education degree from the University of Lethbridge. She is currently the Principal at Piitoayis Family School, Calgary Board of Education. She is author of the book* Omahkitapiksi Okakinikiiwa: Teachings from our Elders *and is a valued author in the collection* Siksikaitsitapi: Stories of the Blackfoot People.

## EXERCISES, CHAPTER FIFTEEN

1. GRATITUDE. "The Sacred Places" is paired with *Gratitude* by Helena Hadala. Grace, humility and compassion are closely aligned. Reflect on all the things you are thankful for in your life and acknowledge the role of others in helping you achieve them. While you are at it, reflect on your own role in recent achievements. Recognize that while others may have helped you along the way, you have also put in hard work and effort to get to where you are. Cultivate a sense of gratitude and humility for your achievement by thanking yourself. Give yourself a reward for something achieved.

2. STORYTELLING. Stoney Nakoda Elder Henry Holloway reminds us that "we all share our stories differently." Tell a different story every day. Even if it is to yourself. Start with two minutes and each day, vary the expression in the story: quiet, passionate, loud, empathetic, using the body, using the face, using the hands, without any movement, one on one, to a group, to your animal companion, include contact, eye contact, no eye contact, or choose your own variation. Enhance this by listening quietly and patiently to someone else's story, connect with them while being quiet.

3. EXPRESS YOURSELF. Iikiinayookaa Marlene stood up for her rights to wear her cowboy boots to school. Have you ever had to stand up to bullies for expressing your personal style? Go ahead and express your style today, or tomorrow, or sometime soon and rejoice in your freedom!

*For further study:*

Grogan, John. *Marley & Me.* HarperCollins, 2005.

Partridge, Lynda. *Lillian & Kokomis: The Spirit of Dance.* Durvile, 2019.

SIXTEEN

# LET THE WORLD CATCH UP

## *Rich Théroux*

∞

*PART 1*

Soaring through the air I hope the giantess is ready to catch me .... She is not. I land hard in a park, tumbling in the wet grass, my body rolls and stops when the back of my head hits a tree. I'm either dead or knocked out. I hope my neck isn't broken. I look awful, so I walk as far away from my mangled body as the rubber band that ties me to it will allow.

It's not too far. Imagine a seven-foot rubber band, I take an eighth step and I snap back toward my mangled body. I turn my back, not wanting to look at it. There are people on the walking path not too far away. If they heard my body thump they did not investigate.

People mind their business this time of night.

I'm sitting,
Sulking. The witch giantess appears.
*I didn't hear your footsteps.*
*How could you without your ears?* she replies
She's right. My ears are still on my body.
Neither of us look at it.

*I guess I'm angry you didn't catch me.*
*What makes you think I didn't catch you?*
I'm without words.

She reaches into a small leather satchel and draws out a pair of gold scissors and snips the thread that binds me to my body.

*Uh, do I need that?*
*You do or you don't.*
*Let's go watch a movie.*

She scoops me up and drops me into her purse.

I don't hear the thumping of her giant footsteps. But I do hear things. She's opened doors—creaky ones. The muffled voice talking to other muffled voices. The smell of popcorn.

She sneaks me out of her purse. Smuggles me into a red and velvet movie theatre. With one hand, she seats me in a pocket on her chest. She hands me a piece of popcorn the size of a beach ball and wipes her hands on her see-through dress. She winks. The lights dim and the film rolls.

Whatever language this film is recorded in is unintelligible. It seems to be a film shot in reverse order telling the narrative of that last two days of my Minotaur friend.

She hands me a pair of paper glasses, one lens red, one lens green. I can't put them on. I left my ears with my body in the park.

*Just try.*

I put the glasses on, somehow they stay in place. Unbelievable. The film is in black and white. The glasses have no effect. I say this and she says, *no matter.* The film is in 4d, height, depth, and time.

*The depth part is only an illusion.*
*Illusions mean nothing here.*
*So where's here?*

This is probably best described at the end. Your end. The opening credits roll backward on screen, then the curtains open, then shut.

*I'm dead?*
*Oh my, don't be so dramatic*
*It's an end it's all the same thing*
*Alpha omega*, I say
She rolls her eye.

Scoops me back into her purse and walks me back to my body. Ties the rubber band. She whispers, *it's shorter now*, stretches me taut and lets go.

With the sting of a rubber band I'm back in my own body. A little stiff. Soggy.

But in contrast.
Everything is quite a bit more…
Vivid.

I walk home chilled from the damp.

I put the key in the latch and open the door. Jess is just getting up. She looks cross. She's not bothered I go out at night. I think she doesn't like waking up alone.

I nod. I close the door.

She's making breakfast and singing. She's an incredibly beautiful singer. She's unbelievably beautiful. She thinks I'm wonderful. I'm not sure if she's a robot spy from space. I'm not sure she's of this Earth. I'm not sure I care.

She is the stuff of science fiction.

I go to my room.

I lost some weight, my new trim build feels 10 years younger. It's improbable. I had to buy new pants. I walk past my couch. I built it. The stereo (a gift). I sit on the bed. I built it. There is art all over the walls. I painted all of it. There are thousands of patched holes in the walls, I patched and covered. I paint, matched the walls in my apartment. They are invisible. They are impossibly invisible.

I put up a shelf, and put a handful of awards on it. I'll patch those holes later on. I wrote in the book I got the awards for that I didn't want any awards.

So it goes.

So, I sit on the bed.
In this story where I have everything I want.
If this were a story, no one would believe it.
How do I write it down without gloating.

And I realized how completely unbelievable it all is.

I'm always terrified to open my eyes.
Humility. That's a part of it
Gratitude. That's another key.

*Where do you go at night?*
*I was in the bra of a giant one-eyed witch.*
Long pause
Long pause
*Is she nice?*
Long pause, and then *sometimes…*

In the hallway, above a very realistic-looking piano and surrounded by paintings, is a whiteboard. I write wishes on it. I erase them as soon as my wishes come true.

Then I wish anew.

Very careful I am with my words, because whatever or whomever it is that grants wishes has a wicked sense of humour.

What am I wishing for this year?
What am I wishing for?

Somewhere, somehow I got the knack for making wishes come true. I'm still ironing out the safest way of asking. You might wish for a rest and be granted the flu. The best way I could describe it is you have to be very careful.

I think in pictures and I tend to think this is key to my luck. As though the wish granters do not speak but they do see. Seeing where you need to be is essential, asking to be there means being somewhere else. And whatever you are ever doing, you are getting ever-better at.

I'm staring at the white board.
I think I might have everything I need.
In the echo chamber of my mind I hear the reverberation, YOU HAVe to moVE.

God I'm scrambled right now, sorry God, didn't mean to blaspheme.

Dear God
I'm feeling
Scrambled
Right now,
Amen.

~

*PART 2*

So now I'm going to tell you about change. Bear with me; it's a little violent.

I do two things for work. In the day I teach; at night I run a street-level art gallery on kind of a shady block.

In school, I feel very vulnerable. There are hundreds of kids with even more hundreds of parents. Each has their own needs, worries, and concerns. Everyone is a little distracted with their own happiness, wellness, and survival.

And I am awkward. So sometimes even my most earnest intentions can be misread. If you think about it, a student getting 50 percent in their classes is only receiving 50 percent of the information. But even a student getting honour grades in the 90th percent is only receiving 9 out of 10 words.

Please - don't - look - at - the - sun - you - could - go - blind.

These are ten words, every once in a while, even your top students might hear.

Please - - look - at - the - sun - you - could - go - blind.

For the most part, if you build the right relationships, the bright ones will ask for clarification before going out to stare at the sun.

Sorry the school bit is a little boring, compared to the one-eyed witches and minotaur moose. But I did promise you a little violence didn't I?

So, there's a new kid in my class.

He's pretty bright and he seems pretty tough, and he smells like cigarettes.

Instinctively, he sits with the two kids who don't do a lot of work in art class and generally sit on the precipice of causing trouble.

I worry about kids who goof off in art class. It's a sign they do nothing at all, or they are planning to grow to be engineers.

My class is large enough that I have a third of the students working outside in the cafeteria. There are tables just outside my door. It's a special privilege to work outside, and I get pummelled by requests to work in the hall at the beginning of every class.

Though I know if I look cross, the kids will avoid asking for anything, so I put on my cross face, take attendance and tell them all to get started on their work because I need to sort some things out.

My art kids open their books or pull out their canvasses and start pounding away.

*Can I borrow you for a second.* I take the new boy out to the hall to give him his sketchbook and get him started. A self portrait is the initiation.

I draw his face, and he is enamoured. Captured.

The rest of the class don't know I'm talking about life; they think I am telling him where his eyes and ears are situated on his face.

There's a large window looking into the room I have to split my mind in two to keep an eye on the class and pay close attention to the new boy's eyes.

*I have this art gallery*, I say. And because this is true, he has no reason to doubt me.

*Right,* he is seeing his face materialize on the paper.

*I have this art gallery and it's street level on a pretty tough block, you get that?*

*Yes,* he says. He cannot take his eyes off his eyes, nose, eyebrow.

*And sometimes it gets a little rough, you see what I am saying?*

And with a nod we agree, it is understood we both understand rough.

*So, I run it with my wife. And outside it's dark. And there's no one to protect me. No parents, no principal, no cops, just me and my wife.*

*Yeah.*

*And about 40 people show up, and I have to keep everyone safe.*

*Yeah.*

*And I have to make everything go my way.*

*Yeah.*

*You ever been outnumbered?*

*Yeah,* he says.

I draw a small brown scar over his eye.

*So how do I do it? It's hard to control 40 people, right?*

Rarely, you meet a kid who really understands the bigger world. So, right away, you know this kid has seen a few things.

*Yeah,* he laughs, *that's a tough one.*

*It's worse than this see? Because sometimes, where we are the door opens and one, or two, sometimes three, even five bad guys roll in. You know what I mean?*

He feels it. *Yeah, I think I do.*

I'm telling the truth and so he has no feeling he should doubt me.

I say, *or once a guy this big came in.* I raise my arm as high as I can. I'm sitting but he understands without asking I'm describing a guy over seven feet tall.

*He outweighed me by a hundred pounds, and he was plastered. You know?*

He looks grim *I know.*

I like this kid a lot for the 25 seconds I've know him.

*So he's just outside this big guy and he's so out of it he takes a spray can out of my wife's hand and he tries to drink out of it.*

The new boy laughs.

*But, I've got to move him away to somewhere safe and all I have is this medium-sized body and my brain. How do I get him to want to go?*

*I don't know, that's a tough one.*

And so I say, because what I am about to tell him is a little complex and not in the curriculum.

*You see it starts with those 40 people. First the door is locked, and I have to open it. I walk inside, me and my little wife, and we start setting things up. In a little bit someone walks in the door. I have to gauge them for mood and personality. Right?*

*Yeah, I get it.*

*So if they are in a good mood, it's three against zero, but if they are not in a good way, it's two against one. I have a few minutes to change their mood or send them away.*

*Right.*

(He sees. This is a future king this one, he really sees the way things ought to be.)

*So, if I get things right when the next person walks in, it's going to be four against zero or three against one. Right?*

*Right.*

*So I do this until it's 10 nothing, If I get to ten, the people in a bad mood will come in and not like it, and usually they leave. I can handle about 40 people if 38 people are in a good mood, you dig?*

*Yeah I dig that.*

He has a new word.

*So, I keep an eye out when it's 38 to two, because I can manage that as long as the bad guys don't roll in.*

*Right, or the really big guy,* and he holds his arm up to indicate a guy about six-and-a-half feet tall.

*Right. Because if it's 38 to two and a big guy rolls in, I'm in trouble. Or if it's 38 to two and five bad guys roll in it's a lot more like seven to one.*

*Just one?*

Exactly.

The motor is rolling and he nods.

*Right,* I say.

*So as long as things are going my way, I've got that whole crowd at my back, it's never seven to one. It's seven to 40,you dig?*

*So they all jump in to help you?*

*No. Never. They are never going to jump in. That never happens. But it's not important. What's important is that it could happen. If things aren't going my way, then I know it can't, won't happen. Could is a very important thing. So what I do is I build the crowd under a set of ideas, or controls, it's called a critical mass.*

*Wait, a what?*

*Doesn't matter* I say, but out of respect I repeat to him slowly: *A critical mass.*

*And then it goes like this.*

*If I've got 40 people in the mass and five bad guys walk in, I know I'm okay. If I have 38 people in the mass and five bad guys walk in, I've got about 2 minutes to heal those 2 people from 38 to 40.*

*Either way when I walk over to the five bad guys, or the one really big bad guy I just need to believe that he, or they are going to go away.*

*Oh, yeah,* he says, and he laughs as though I just gave him the keys to the kingdom.

*You picking up what I'm putting down?*

*I dig.*

So, I say, *Uh, hey you know, you can't be here, I can help you, but I can't help you right now. You need to go and come back later. You're always welcome here, but not right now. And they go.* I cock one eye.

*I dig, I really do.*

*So as long as I believe what I am saying, they go.*

*Yeah.*

*You believe me?*

*I do.*

*Good.*

*So it was 38 to 1 in there last week and now its 38 to two.*
*You got me?*
*I do.*

He and I walk back into class.
And then it's 39 to 2
And 40 to one
And finally 41 to zero.

And we all draw.
We manifest with our most powerful imaginations.

Until the bell rings.

~

*DENOUEMENT*

I step into the hall and I pass one of the new teachers.

*How's your day?*
*Not good*, she says.
*You need some magic?*
*Sure.*

I put my hand in my pocket and I sprinkle some magic dust in her hand. She looks puzzled and I say, don't spill it, put it in your hair. She smiles, I've cheered her up, and she pantomimes putting magic dust in her hair and she tears up a little.

I sigh. That was a waste.

One of my students sees and looks at me earnestly.
I don't have much. I do not want to waste it.

She puts her hand out.
I dip into my pocket.
I scatter what's left of my magic in her hand.
Her hand dips. It is much heavier than it looks.
She carries it to her head and works it into her hair.
The particles affix to her imagination.

*Besides being a caveman, Rich Théroux is a genius talent at painting and drawing. His art hangs here and there in prominent homes and galleries but he prefers not to boast about it. Rich is founder of Calgary's Rumble House gallery and happens to also teach junior high school art. He is the author and illustrator of* Stop Making Art and Die: A Survival Guide for Artists, *co-author of the poetry book,* A Wake in the Undertow, *along with his partner Jess Théroux (Szabo), and author and illustrator of the award-winning The* River Troll: A Story About Love.

## EXERCISES, CHAPTER SIXTEEN

1. PATIENCE. "Let the World Catch Up" is paired with *Patience* by Helena Hadala. In Rich's story, the hero tries out 4D glasses that he feels has no effect, but when he removes them, "Everything is quite a bit more…Vivid." Close your eyes patiently for about a minute, and when you open them, look at the world around you like you are seeing it for the first time. What do you see more vividly than ever before?

2. ACHIEVEMENTS. The author's intentions are closely tied with success with his students and also with his gallery patrons. Choose something simple and rewarding that you have already achieved and practice visualizing this successful intention for two minutes. You may wish to draw it, dance it, write a poem, or see it in your mind's eye. Do you have a previously unobtained intention that might be achievable? Visualize this in your mind's eye—or draw it, dance it, or write a poem. Fully accept your achievement without any negativity.

3. CREATIVE IMPULSES. Rich's hero sprinkles magic dust on the outstretched hands of two people, one who is not ready for its magic and just pretends, and one whose imagination is about to be titillated. Extend your hands, inhale deeply to receive the magic dust. Your hand dips because it is heavier than you think. Rub your face and work the magic into your hair. Which of your creative impulses becomes inspired?

*For further study:*

Eliot, Alexander. *Sight and Insight.* New York, Harcourt Brace Jovanovich, 1978.

Gaiman, Neil, and Chris Riddell. *Art Matters: Because Your Imagination Can Change the World.* Headline, 2018.

## "For Further Study" Collated

*These are the resources listed by the authors and editors throughout the book for your further consideration and study.*

Adler, Janet. *Offering from the Conscious Body: The Discipline of Authentic Movement.* Inner Traditions, 2002.

Anthony, Mark. *The Afterlife Frequency: The Scientific Proof of Spiritual Contact and How That Awareness Will Change Your Life.* Llewellyn, 2021.

Blackie, Sharon. *Foxfire, Wolfskin and Other Stories of Shapeshifting Women.* September Publishing, 2019.

Brennan, Barbara Ann. *Core Light Healing: My Personal Journey and Advanced Concepts for Creating the Life You Long to Live.* Hay House, 2017.

Butler Bass, Diana. *Grateful: The Transformative Power of Giving Thanks.* HarperOne, 2018.

Cameron, Julia. *The Artist's Way: A Spiritual Path to Higher Creativity.* TarcherPerigee, 2002.

Castaneda, Carlos. *The Art of Dreaming.* HarperCollins, 1993.

Chödrön, Pema. *How We Live Is How We Die.* Shambhala Publications, 2022.

Eliot, Alexander. *Sight and Insight.* New York, Harcourt Brace Jovanovich, 1978.

Gaiman, Neil, and Chris Riddell. *Art Matters: Because Your Imagination Can Change the World.* Headline, 2018.

Goldman, Jonathan and Andi Goldman. *The Humming Effect.* Healing Arts Press, 2017, Rochester, VT.

Heinlein, Robert A. *Have Space Suit, Will Travel.* Scribner, 1958.

Jung, Carl. *The Archetypes and the Collective Unconscious.* Princeton University Press, 1981.

Kaplan, Janice. *The Gratitude Diaries: How a Year Looking on the Bright Side Can Transform Your Life.* Penguin Books, 2016.

King, Stephen. *Rose Madder*. Viking, 1995.

Mackesy, Charlie. *The Boy, the Mole, the Fox and the Horse.* HarperOne, 2019.

Matthiessen, Peter. *In the Spirit of Crazy Horse*. Penguin Books, 1992.

McKusick, Eileen Day. *Tuning the Biofield: Healing with Vibrational Sound Therapy.* Healing Arts Press, 2014.

Medicine Eagle, Brooke. *The Last Ghost Dance: A Guide for Earth Mages.* Bear & Company, 2000.

Mountain, Antoine, *Child of Morning Star.: Embers of an Ancient Dawn.* Durvile, 2022.

Orwell, George. *1984.* Secker and Warburg, 1949.

Partridge, Lynda. *Lillian & Kokomis: The Spirit of Dance.* Durvile, 2019.

Redfield, James. *The Celestine Prophecy.* Warner Books, 1993.

Richardson, Cheryl. *The Art of Extreme Self Care: Transform Your Life One Month at a Time.* Hay House, 2009.

Storm, Hyemeyohsts. *Seven Arrows.* Harper Perennial, 1991.

Talaga, Tanya. *Seven Fallen Feathers.* House of Anansi Press, 2017.

Taylor, Drew Hayden. *The Night Wanderer.* Annick Press, 2007.

Virtue, Doreen. *Angels 101: An Introduction To Connecting, Working, and Healing With The Angels.* Hay House, 2006.

Wagamese, Richard. *Embers.* Douglas & McIntyre, 2016.

Wallis, Christopher D. *Tantra Illuminated: The Philosophy, History, and Practice of a Timeless Tradition.* Mattamayura Press, 2012.

DURVILE & UPROUTE BOOKS

DURVILE.COM

## "Every River Lit" Series

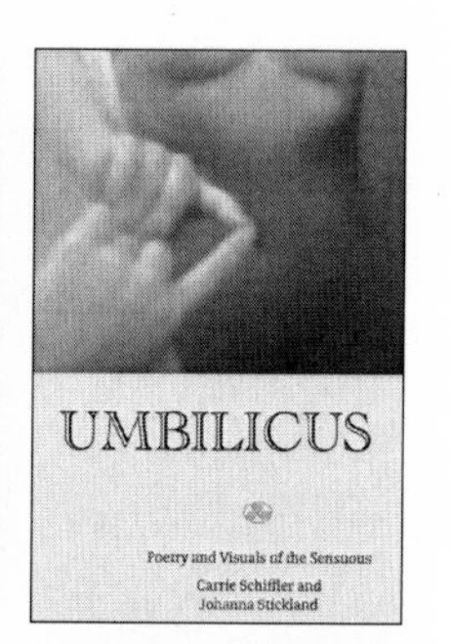

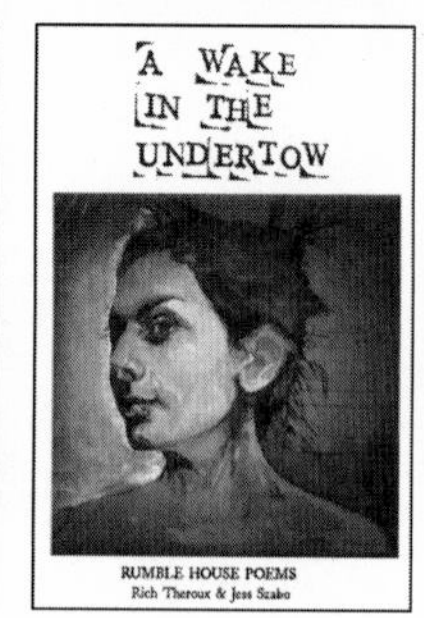

## DURVILE & UPROUTE BOOKS

DURVILE.COM

# "Ways of Light" Titles

Durvile & UpRoute Books, a small-but-mighty Canadian indie press, publishes print books, e-books, audiobooks, and rich multimedia for enhancement of meaning. Our vision is to inspire authors and artists to bring new knowledge to the world.

## About the Editors, Artist, and Foreword Writer

**Editor Julian Hobson** CHt BHSC was born in Sheffield, UK, inheriting and developing the abilities of healing through his grandmother. He lives on the western slopes of the Rockies in the East Kootenays of B.C., sharing his time between his profession as a cardiac sonographer, his practice of hypnotherapy, and nature.

**Editor Lorene Shyba** MFA PhD is publisher and creative director at Durvile & UpRoute Books. She has brought her academic rigour to nurture the evolvements, exercises, and multimedia of this book, alongside her gifted project colleagues. She lives in the foothills of the Rockies, near Diamond Valley, Alberta.

**Artist Helena Hadala** MFA RCA is an artist whose practice focuses on imagery that reflects her perceptual world. Zen Buddhism and Taoism have informed her life and creative process. Helena is an elected member of the Royal Canadian Academy of the Arts and she lives in Calgary, Alberta.

**Foreword writer Elizabeth Rockenbach** BIP is an advanced Barbara Brennan School of Healing practitioner, and a faculty member at the BBSH School in NYC. She is also co-founder of Universal-Healing.org. Elizabeth lives in her "Sunflower Home" in New Mexico.